TOUCHSTONE

LEVERAGING TODAY'S PSYCHOLOGICAL SMOG

by LINKEDIN AND TOWN HALL ACHIEVER OF THE YEAR
EY NOMINEE ENTREPRENEUR OF THE YEAR
GRAND HOMAGE LYS DIVERSITY

Dr. BAK NGUYEN, DMD

&

by AMERICAN ASSOCIATION OF MEMORIAL AWARD IN RESEARCH
GEORGE W. SWITZER MEMORIAL AWARD

Dr. KEN SEROTA, DDS, MMSc

TO ALL PROFESSIONALS LOOKING TO HEAL, COPE
AND PERFORM UNDER CONSTANT STRESS AND EVER
HIGHER STANDARDS. UNDERSTAND AND LEVERAGE.

by Dr. BAK NGUYEN

ISBN: 978-1-989536-53-7

ABOUT THE AUTHORS

From Canada, **Dr BAK NGUYEN**, Nominee EY Entrepreneur of the year, Grand Homage LYS DIVERSITY, and LinkedIn & TownHall Achiever of the year. Dr Bak is a cosmetic dentist, CEO and founder of Mdex & Co. His company is revolutionizing the dental field. Speaker and motivator, he wrote more than 70 books in 35 months accumulating many world records (to be officialized). He is on the quest to set the next word record of writing 72 books / 36 months. His books are covering:

- **ENTREPRENEURSHIP**
- **LEADERSHIP**
- **QUEST OF IDENTITY**
- **DENTISTRY AND MEDICINE**
- **PARENTING**
- **CHILDREN BOOKS**
- **PHILOSOPHY**

In 2003, he founded Mdex, a dental company upon which in 2018, he launched the most ambitious private endeavour to reform the dental industry, Canada wide. Philosopher, he has close to his heart the quest of happiness of the people surrounding him, patients and colleagues alike. In 2020, he launched an International collaborative initiative named **THE ALPHAS** to share knowledge and to Entrepreneurs and Doctors to thrive through the Greatest Pandemic and Economic depression of our time.

These projects have allowed Dr Nguyen to attract interests from the international and diplomatic community and he is now the center of a global discussion in the wellbeing and the future of the health profession. It is in that matter that he shares his thoughts and encourages the health community to share their own stories.

"It's not worth it go through it alone! Together, we stand, alone, we fall."

Motivational speaker and serial entrepreneur, philosopher and author, from his own words, Dr Nguyen describes himself as a dentist by circumstances, an entrepreneur by nature and a communicator by passion.

He also holds recognitions from the Canadian Parliament and the Canadian Senate.

From Canada, **Dr. KEN SEROTA**, DDS, MMSc, graduated from the University of Toronto Faculty of Dentistry in 1973 and received his Certificate in Endodontics and Master of Medical Sciences degree from the Harvard-Forsyth Dental Center in Boston, Massachusetts. He was awarded the George W. Switzer Memorial Award for excellence in prosthodontics in 1973. In 1981, he was awarded the American Association of Memorial Award in Research. In 1987 he was awarded the Ontario Dental Association for contribution to continuing education.

In 2000, he founded ROOTS, the first online Endodontic forum and coordinated the first ROOTS Summit. In 2004, in concert with Oemus Media, he founded the Roots Journal. In 2015 he founded NEXUS, in order to integrate all dental disciplines. Contributing editor to Endodontic Practice, he has published over 70 articles and has lectured internationally on endodontics and implants. He is the Global Director of Social Media and Marketing for Navident and is a clinical instructor in the University of Toronto postdoctoral endodontics department.

Dr. Serota is a member of : Ontario Dental Association, Halton Peel Dental Association, Canadian Dental Association, Ontario Society of Endodontists, American Association of Endodontists, Alpha Omega Fraternity, Digital Dental Society.

He coordinates the annual Run for the Cure event, to bring an end to cancer.

TOUCHSTONE

LEVERAGING TODAY'S PSYCHOLOGICAL SMOG

by Dr. BAK NGUYEN
& Dr. KEN SEROTA

INTRODUCTION
by Dr. BAK NGUYEN

These are the first official words that I am writing since I last broke the world record of writing 72 books over a period of 36 months, a little more than two months ago. Looking to set that record, I ended up scoring a few more on the way.

At the end of June 2020, I realized that I had to write a book every 8 days for 8 weeks straight to complete that titanic challenge. Well, I announced it on social media and never looked back.

By the 3rd week of August, I was done, with 10 days in advance! What a journey! Well, not quite. From the end of July to the end of August 2020, Amazon published 6 of my latest books.

So as the record was about writing 72 books over 36 months, I ended up publishing a book every 8 days on average for 8 weeks straight… with 10 days to spare. How many world records did I just set?

I must say that it was both exciting and exhausting. I took those 10 days break, only to jump on new projects as completing the first **UAX** (Ultimate Audio Experience) and using my newest protocols to produce audiobooks in parallel with my writing.

Well, by September, **HORIZON volume 3** was submitted and approved for streaming on Spotify. We are still waiting for Apple Music to confirm, but since, it is not a first, we do expect good news.

Streaming is not podcasting. Everyone with motivation and something to say can start a podcast but streaming, that's the major league! That's the artists' league. To me, it is my entrance into pop culture and popular trends.

Well, as I was googling my name to see the links of my newest album on the web, I discovered by accident the greatest of fortune! My name shows up in Barnes and Noble's website. Barnes and Noble!!!

This is a huge victory. Until now, I was still seen as a self-published author and a loner. For reason that I do not fully comprehend, to self-publish isn't prestigious enough. I tried the traditional ways, but waiting for rejection and approbation is simply not my style. While waiting, I kept producing…

To be featured at Barnes and Noble is a tremendous recognition, one that is moving my core as an author and one that should give hope to all of us, looking for our voice.

Barnes and Noble are, by far, the biggest bookstores chain in the USA with 5 Billion in annual sale. This does not mean that I will be an overnight bestseller, but it means that I have reached the major leagues, on my own, not looking back.

Barnes and Noble accepted 12 of my latest titles, meaning that they have picked up on Dr. Bak's phenomenon. What a great surprise. That was my way to celebrate my latest world record in style, from Barnes and Noble's website!

I posted it on my social media and the web went on fire! As my co-authors were celebrating our new victory, I did as I always do, I moved on. What's next?

> "I wrote 1.16 million words so you won't have to."
> Dr. Bak Nguyen

Yup, those were my words. 1.16 million of them. As I set new world records, one after the next, I was looking to know how I could beat the light speed. Writing with William 2 years ago got me to break the sound barrier, going from 15 books over 15 months to 36 books over 18 months + 1 week.

How about embracing my laziness and giving it value? How? Well, how about noting writing anymore and keep scoring more titles? And this is how I came up with the idea of the **Apollo protocol**.

It took me a few weeks to put together my own intelligence, experience writing books and the power of AI, artificial intelligence to give birth to a new way to share stories and knowledge: **APOLLO**.

In short, I packaged my structure and storytelling experience into forms and questions for an interview. Within 3-4 hours interviews, answering the tailored-made questions, the material is then transcribed into a manuscript and edited.

Then, we return the manuscript to the author for reading and correction before the final editing process. With my protocols, I can get a 10-15k words book from a 3 hours interview and, within a month, have it available for paperback order on Amazon!

A month, this is insane! But there is even better. The best part is that the author will only have put 3 hours for the interview, 1 hour to prepare for that interview, and the time to read and correct his or her own manuscript. Even if the author is a slow reader, within 20 hours, the reading should be done.

That brings us to have a book ready within 24 hours of work and within a month with the right protocols and team in place! How about that for a new world record?

The **APOLLO protocol**, I built it for myself, to keep the fun in the race. But then, the reality of COVID caught me. Having to cover my commercial rent for the 3 months of confinement was a very, very hard pill to swallow. Thanks to my team, we successfully did so, but it made me realize how fragile our equilibrium is.

That's when I decided to swallow my pride and to share my best tools for the world to enjoy. I will be helping people to find their voice and empowering them with great tools, hoping to see someone beat me at my own game. That is how I will keep my relevancy!

It is in the midst of that excitement that I met Dr. Ken Serota. Ken invited me for an interview. As my habits of saying YES are still very predominant, I accepted without hesitation. Then, Ken started to make more and more research on my work and my accomplishments. He pushed it all out within a 90 minutes interview.

Ken is a great host. I never looked as cool and as accomplished as how he painted me on his show. Needless to say that our friendship started instantly as we were on the air.

Within that live interview, he forced my hand (very gently) to be part of his medical entrepreneurship community and was hoping for my contribution. I said YES.

Then, to better comprehend my involvement, I turned the table and invited him for an interview on the **ALPHASHOW**, my show. It is within that second interview that our friendship was sealed.

Like-minded, compassionate, and gentle, Ken inspired me to open up and to share more and more. Not just ideas, but resources too. As we are both worried about the present COVID crisis and its mental toll on the population, the idea of writing a book to cope on stress during COVID time became a project.

Well, you know me. I am too lazy to keep projects laying around in my head. 2 weeks later, I embraced the air again on the **ALPHASHOW** to brainstorm and kickstart the writing of our book: **TOUCHSTONE, LEVERAGING TODAY'S PSYCHOLOGICAL SMOG.**

"Changing the world from a dental chair."
Dr. Bak Nguyen

That was Ken's favorite quote of mine. So let's do it, let's change the world, as 2 dentists. As Ken is embracing this process as groundwork for his thesis (yes, at 70, he is starting the process of a Ph.D.), Ken will be very meticulous and analytical about the different kinds of stress we are facing in today's environment.

As for me, I am Dr. Bak. That's the only way I know how to perform. I will be sharing with you my perspective about stress and how to leverage it to victory.

"Success is a state of mind."

I wish I could sign that quote, but someone smarter beat me to it. That being said, I can't agree more. Together, Ken and I, we will map stress and its derivatives, we will try to feel and to understand stress from different perspectives and to address it.

We may not have all the answers, but we will tell you what we would do facing that pressure and those odds.

Through these troubled times, may our works and words help you find comfort and hope. The hope to reinvent yourself, the hope that tomorrow can be better, the hope that we can all grow from this unfortunate event.

This is **TOUCHSTONE**, leveraging today's psychological smog.

STRESS is part of life, for better and for worse.
Better since it can be leveraged
Worse, if it is in control
Dr. BAK NGUYEN

CHAPTER 1

LABELING STRESS

by Dr. BAK NGUYEN

What is stress, really? At its core, stress is a stimulus conducting the message that change is coming. Is that change a threat? Often, to most people, any change is a threat by default. And here comes the bad labeling attached to stress.

A rapid google search about what is stress will show you different definitions as: being unable to cope and underwhelmed, emotional and physical tension, natural defence against predators, natural body's response… and that's just within the first page of results.

If you dig a little, you will find out that we each have our own definition of stress. Most people will label it as bad, and some, to distinguish themselves, will paint it as good, explaining their reasoning with many, many words…

This aren't theories, but opinions. Maybe this is how we came up with so many definitions and remedies for stress, and yet, it is still a big part of our lexicon and way of life.

Let's go back a little bit, to the fight or flight reaction. It is now well known that we are hardwired with these reflexes as we face imminent danger. Facing danger, our body will mobilize all of its resources to maximize our odds of surviving.

Will it be through a fight to the death or running as fast as possible far from danger? That's a decision coming from our mindset and training. But basically, it doesn't matter much, since our body will have produced the same hormones to mobilize our mental and physical attributes. Adrenaline and cortisol are the primary stress hormones produced.

Adrenaline will increase blood pressure and heart rate to boost the available energy. Cortisol will increase the sugar level to increase brain awareness and decrease all immediate non-essential systems as digestive, immune system response, and sexual system.

If you look at the responses, it should shed some light on most illnesses that we, as modern societies, are facing. Does that mean that our body is broken? Not at all!

Our body was built to give us the most chance to survive. The hormonal response to stress is, in its nature, a short term reaction, so we can fight for our lives or run for it. Well, the change (or danger) has changed nowadays. The change is not punctual anymore as we do not need to fight or run for our lives, but it has become a way to respond to any change of our exterior and interior environment.

"Life is dynamic, moving, always morphing, and never standing still. If not, we wouldn't be calling it Life."
Dr. Bak Nguyen

So the real issue here is how are we facing Life and its evolution? By definition, Life is change. If our reaction to change is stress, does it means that we are threatened by Life itself? If that's the case, we have barely scratched the surface with our stress and emotional distress.

"Fighting Life or running from it, where would it lead?
To the opposite of Life..."
Dr. Bak Nguyen

And this is often how we choose to see stress and react to it. Stress is a stimulus, nothing more and nothing less. As the danger is gone, so should our hormones and mindsets. Easier said than done, will you tell me. And you are absolutely right.

But if we can agree on the fact that stress is a stimulus to changes, and that it will cascade a physiological and hormonal reaction with known symptoms, now we have a chance to tweak the system.

We can either tweak our sensibility to interpret what is stress and its required level to ignite our flight-or-fight response. Know that hormonal response is all or nothing. There is no such thing as a half response. It is either we are filled with adrenaline and cortisol or we are not. That is how our human bodies are built.

> "Fighting our body will simply be a waste of energy.
> Accepting it will give us an edge."
> Dr. Bak Nguyen

So what do you see as stressful and to what degree will ultimately affect our reaction to stress and the release of the stress hormones? And this is where mindset, culture, and training will have a huge impact on someone's behavior and even personality.

This is what we, Ken and I, will be looking for, those touchstones that tricker your stress level to the roof and find ways for you to not step on those touchstones too often.

Why don't we eliminate those touchstones? Well, many disciplines and cultures have that expertise, to exorcise fear and demons with fire. The cleansing ritual is often worse than the bad it trying to fight.

I am not a believer of such methods, but being raised as a catholic, I have my share of understanding cleansing, fire, and sacrifice. If I came to elevate myself, so today you deem worthy of your time to read my words and thoughts, well I successfully freed myself, not with amputation and cleansing, but from acceptance, compassion, and understanding.

Our modern societies see Diversity as a high value and a new trend. Well, I applied the same principle to myself, accepting the good and the less. Actually, after a while, I do not see good or bad anymore, I see myself and what I prefer.

Rest assured, this is merely the beginning of our journey together, we will come back to fear, stress, good and bad. For now, just accept that we are so full of labels that burden our awareness and understanding of ourselves.

I wrote several books about the personal **QUEST OF IDENTITY**, I know plenty about burden, awareness, and choices. This book is about stress, especially the kind of stresses we each experience in challenging times.

Well, what better opportunity to dig in and to understand what is so obvious and in front of our eyes. At this stage, who amongst us are still in denial? Are you stressed by the COVID crisis?

As a dentist, I never saw so many jaws related pain or broken teeth due to bruxism. Minor problems if we understand the crisis that Humanity is facing right now. Fix the tooth, give them a night guard and move on…

This would be such an error not to address the deeper and underlining issues. Not stress, since change is bigger and happening faster and faster than ever, but how we interpret that change and choose to do with the rise of hormonal response from stress.

The easiest answer would be to give nature its course. Go on and run until your body purge the adrenaline and cortisol from your system. Then, you will go hungry and boost your appetite. Even your sexual hormones might awake. That should ease your stress…

But within today's crisis, it is simply not enough to purge the hormones, since it will come back up soon enough. So what else can one do? How about embracing change instead of fighting it or running from it?

"I am too lazy to spend my life running from something.
I prefer to run towards that something.
It is the shorter way."
Dr. Bak Nguyen

I told you how lazy I am. Fighting is too much work and fleeing, well, it is even a longer engagement. I have struck down most of the labels about stress. Today, I look at it as a stimulus, nothing more and nothing less. Some stimuli are bigger and bolder, some are more subtle. Those are facts, not judgments and certainly, I try not to attach any emotions to the variance of stimuli.

The first question I trained myself with is how do I interpret that stimulus. This takes time and training, but eventually, I came to master my emotions not to interfere and to see stress, at least, most of the stresses, as stimuli.

If my body responds to it, so be it. I am powerless to stop my own hormones from surging. Denying my hormones and their responses will be an even greater mistake. I learned to follow the flow.

On that, allow me to elaborate. As my hormones are surging, I know that my body deems the change important enough to mobilize my abilities. Then, I use those abilities to analyze and to react to the change in question.

Like you, most of the change that I face, I do not have the power to overturn them. I can fight them, ignore them, or try to flee. Well, fighting, as I said, is too much work for me. Ignoring them is even a worse bargain since the repercussions to my body and mental health are even worse. How about fleeing? I don't like running.

"And in COVID times, fleeing is pretty limited.
So I decided to embrace a fourth alternative: to leverage."
Dr. Bak Nguyen

At the beginning of COVID, I was (and still am) at the head of a dental company with the promise to change the world. Yes, a dental company, **Mdex & Co**. We were expanding when COVID first hit us.

Then, the confinement followed. As the dental industry, we were the first to be shut down, 2 to 3 weeks prior to anyone else. We obeyed. Needless to tell you the financial burden and the headache to keep the company afloat.

Confined home, I was under enormous stress. Every time the prime minister had a speech, it was about the immediate future of the citizen… my future. Even with influence, I was powerless about my own fate.

My choices were either to wait for the next announcement that might give me a heart attack or to rebel. There was nowhere to flee. Well, this is where I noticed that I was still battling with the labels.

Since I had no power over my faith and the events, I decided that it wasn't my concern anymore. Yes, I said that out loud as I was showering one morning. I went out, got dressed, powered on my computer and went online. I went online because it the only place that I wasn't confined and limited.

I connected with different people. I learned what ZOOM is and mastered it quickly. I brought my art of movie making and narrative to it and I discovered a new facet of myself. I quickly rose as a world anchor in my field.

I had no idea what I was doing, but from one interview to the next, looking for solutions to this crisis, I made new powerful friends from like-minded people. From one summit to the next, we came to influence some national decisions about our profession.

I wasn't fighting nor dictating anything, I was connecting and shedding the light at. Today, we have come to be known as the **ALPHAS**. Independent thinkers and shakers, actors of the economy, and of the dental industry, coming together to help shape the future... or at least, to help prepare for what is ahead.

I started connecting with one dentist, then two and six and ten. I forced the hand of a few friends, presidents of companies, and we came together. I pushed my mentors and they joined too. Lately, I even had the privilege to interview **RON KLEIN**, an American iconic innovator who created the magnetic strip behind the credit card, created MLS (multi listing services), and digitalized the Wall Street bond market.

Mr. Klein was very generous of his time. He accepted the interview because, now more than ever, we need the hope and inspiration to reinvent ourselves. Well, that was his response to this stimulus. A challenge, sure, but the opportunity to reinvent ourselves.

Amongst my friends and guests, some have created billions in value, most have created millions. Some are political leaders and some have led world change innovations.

They all have accepted my invitation to join the **ALPHAS** and to share their perspective and secret to leverage themselves out of this crisis. More than that, we are in contact and are exchanging ideas to rebuild our industries and societies, off-air.

I do not lead nor own any of them. I simply eased the connection and the exchange of ideas. That's how I became a world anchor, from the confinement in my living room.

Well, only the future will tell, but some of the ideas discussed have the potential to get us back further ahead and higher than we were before the COVID war began. I am not talking about personal gain only, but about projects that might make the world a better place to all.

Those are still ideas and projects. But if you know who is stirring them, you too will have hope. As for myself, well, I am Dr. Bak and way too lazy to have projects and ideas laying around. Those ideas with merits will have my involvement.

From scoring the world record of 72 books over 36 months, I went to score a few on the side writing a book every 8 days for 8 weeks, straight. That's the kind of involvement and commitment I can bring to the table.

So from the stress of COVID to the inability to fight and having nowhere to flee, I got rid of the labels. I leveraged instead. You too can let go of your labels and liabilities. What's not in your control is simply not your burden to carry.

Try it, and see how different you feel already. You will feel lighter, taller, and stronger. Now, what to do with that renewed strength is your choice. The stimulus just woke you up. Now the fun begins.

"Just like your hormones, there is no half response.
Don't amputate, embrace fully."
Dr. Bak Nguyen

This is **TOUCHSTONE**, leveraging today's psychological smog.

STRESS is part of life, for better and for worse.
Better since it can be leveraged
Worse, if it is in control
Dr. BAK NGUYEN

CHAPTER 2

RESILIENCE AND COPING

by Dr. KEN SEROTA

We are forever facing challenges in our lives, they drive us, motivate us, define us, and give substance to our very existence. We must cope with these challenges, meet them head-on in order to defend ourselves from them. They can drain us of our strength, our will, our energy.

However, we can train our bodies and our minds to be resilient. It is important to distinguish between **resilience** and **coping**.

Resilience influences how an event is appraised and influences the stress process at multiple stages. We process and appraise these stressors based on experience, the history of meta-cognitions in response to the constellation of emotions that have engaged us in the past, and the results of our coping strategies both reactive and unreactive.

Every day of our lives requires us to cope with one thing or another. The drivers on the way to work, the staff person who is off their game, the boss who lets their personal or work stress control their leadership abilities, our children, our friends, our spouse or partners are all part of a fabric of stress that envelopes our day.

Coping is the process by which we expend conscious effort and energy to solve our personal and interpersonal problems. In the case of stress, coping mechanisms seek to master, minimize, or tolerate stress and stressors that occur in everyday life.

Coping skills or strategies are adaptive goals of reducing or dealing with stress, but some strategies can actually be maladaptive (unhealthy) or merely ineffective. It is the distinction between the two that make all the difference.

How do we deal with irrational behaviors, a child acting out? How do we deal with criticism, unjustified, or justified? How do we deal with confrontation, conflict, what we hear and see on the news, from reliable friends?

Where is the baseline, is it a constant, does it vary for every circumstance. Do we address stress from a balanced position, with positivity or negativity? How do we know we are demonstrating an accurate response, a true response, a valid response, and in what context?

Maladaptive behaviors are those that inhibit a person's ability to adjust to particular situations. This type of behavior is often used to reduce one's anxiety, but the result is dysfunctional and non-productive. How often are we pushed to the limit, or pushed to exceed it?

"How often do we let others euphemistically "rent space in our heads?"
Dr. Ken Serota

What others think of us is none of our business, but how quick can we respond when stress is immediate, are we sufficiently grounded to be reflexive and avoid the proverbial gut kick?

The term "coping" usually refers to dealing with the stress that comes after a stressor is presented, but many people also use proactive coping strategies to eliminate or avoid stressors before they occur.

What do we base these strategies on? Do our past successes, what we read, who we have encountered in stressful situations, make our response transferable? How does our day during it's transition from sunrise to sunset establish **thresholds of tolerance**?

Life is an endless array of questions and answers, but are they the right answers, or are we so stressed that the answers we provide are misguided or misdirected?

How we cope and the strategies we used are determined by personality traits and type, social context, and the nature of the stressor involved. Are we the same person in different social settings, who do we enjoy engaging with, who do we find intolerable, who intimidates us, is there a type?

When faced with adversity in life, how do we adapt? Why do some people seem to bounce back from tragic events or loss much more quickly than others? Why do some people seem to get "stuck" at a point in their life, without the ability to move forward?

"We need to learn to be resilient in order to cope."
Dr. Ken Serota

When faced with a tragedy, natural disaster, health concern, relationship disruption, work, or school problems, resilience is how well a person can adapt to these events.

The COVID-19 pandemic is an existential threat. Our lives have for most of us have been living in relative comfort. By and large, we do not suffer deprivation, we are healthy or can find resources to resolve health issues.

"COVID is both a Trojan horse and a frontal assault on our very existence and sense of self and psychological well-being."
Dr. Ken Serota

A person with good resilience has the ability to bounce back more quickly and with less stress than someone whose resilience is less developed. Everybody has resilience. It's just a question of how much and how well you put it to good use in your life.

Resilience doesn't mean the person doesn't feel the intensity of the event or problem. Instead, it just means that they've found a pretty good way of dealing with it more quickly than others. To each their own?

What if our resilience is manifested in negative ways; smoking, overeating, drugs, alcohol, addictive behaviors that alleviate in the short term but bring long term consequences?

Everyone can learn to increase their resilience abilities. Like any human skill, learning greater resilience is something that you can do at any age, from any background, no matter your education or family relationships.

However, what if we are the product of an environment where coping was expressed in a damaging manner? Overzealous parents, whose resilience tended to negative traits, mockery, denigration, racist overtones, us versus them mentality, what if they established the guiding principles of our resilience.

"All you need to do in order to increase your resilience
is to have the willingness to do so."
Dr. Ken Serota

Then seek out ways of learning more about resilience, either from search engines (or with the help of a trained behavior specialist, like a psychologist). And yet, the elephant in the room always remains as our emotional well-being, our mental health. What if we learn to be resilient with anger to push away the perceived danger, or physical violence, coping by lashing out?

We can teach ourselves the strategies for both **coping** and **resilience**, the ability to bounce back stronger through exercise, making time for solitude, engaging in positive self-talk, aspiring to greater heights of experience in our lives, learning from failure, and most importantly, cultivating both humor and curiosity, nature's tranquilizers.

"Our expectations of self must be realistic."
Dr. Ken Serota

We can distract ourselves when threatened. Is the fear real, are we mind-reading? Do we think only in black and white? Do we distract ourselves to avoid the direct threat? How do we manage our hostile feelings?

Do we meditate to prepare our days? Are we in the moment? Are we mindful? Do we rest between high-stress periods with systematic relaxation procedures? Are the coping and resilient arrows in our quiver used effectively?

Build your resilience and coping by having a positive view of yourself and confidence in your strengths and abilities. Make the effort to make **realistic plans**, and then begin the work to carry them out with effect.

Assess how effectively you manage feelings and impulses with communication skills or good problem-solving skills.

"We are endlessly a work in progress
and therein lies all the difference."
Dr. Ken Serota

This is **TOUCHSTONE**, leveraging today's psychological smog.

STRESS is part of life, for better and for worse.
Better since it can be leveraged
Worse, if it is in control
Dr. BAK NGUYEN

CHAPTER 3

EATING STRESS DAILY

by Dr. BAK NGUYEN

I promised you that we would be walking in different shoes to feel the different kinds of stresses, and to understand the different situations. Well, let's start with ours, as dentists.

Are we stressed people? Yes, we have the stress of being medical doctors, putting the needs of the other before our own. We have the burden to not have the right to error which set each of us on a collision course with the laws of statistic.

Playing the medical game, the odds are against us: no one can hope for the perfect score, if he or she is practicing for a long time.

"Perfection is a lie."
Dr. Bak Nguyen

Then, most of us have the financial burden of running a small hospital with all of its departments, but without much resources, preparation nor management training. And we succeed to thrive. How? Because we are comparing ourselves to the other guy and the spirit of competition manages to keep us afloat.

But then, as competition is keeping our head out of the water, we often isolate ourselves, being the king or queen of a tiny hill and surrounding ourselves, not with peers, but with underlinks. Please mark my words, I am not taking anything away from the team members, without them, there would be no clinic.

But to be obeyed daily without much challenge is hardly a way to evolve gracefully. In other words, we are losing our competitive edge and our sharpness slowly. That's another stress to face, eventually.

As we are the commanding officer in the operatory and maybe our clinic, outside of these specific parameters, the roles are reversed. We are loyal soldiers to our governing bodies and licensing boards. We obey without the right to question. This is yet another stress that we are submitting ourselves to.

Do I even have to start describing the stress of managing a team? To recruit, to form, to manage? To hire and to fire? And this is done after we have punched out the clock on our surgeries. How efficient is our process? Forget efficiency, is this even humanly sustainable? Stress over stress over more stress.

And what about furniture and keeping up with the trends, new methods, and the market? Again, it is a new race each time. And every single time, it is a survival race. Our only guideline to compare ourselves to the norm is the average, and to readjust from there.

Is this an accurate portrait of what it is to be a dentist nowadays? Not really. Those are merely the side effects of being a dentist in modern times. The true reality of dentistry is that, as we operate on people who are fully awake and aware, we are absorbing the stress of each patient.

This is what we signed up for, as doctors. But never it has been said that we had to absorb the stress of our patients while performing surgical perfection.

And somehow, we did that successfully repeatedly. Then, with false confidence, what do we do? We stack up our schedule with more and more patients.

More patients mean more stress to absorb. More patients is more income, but also more expenses as the team has to grow: more infrastructures, more equipments, more liabilities. But since the average is doing it, so are we.

What kind of life does that result into? All the stress absorbed, all the side stress coming with the practice, the perfection, the comparison, the financial burden, the management, and the pride to succeed are all adding up. How do we cope?

We know that stress is a biological stimulus that will release hormones, **ADRENALINE** and **CORTISOL**. The easiest way was to go for a run and to flush out those stress hormones from our system.

As we are stacking up our schedule, which leads to more administrative work after operation hours, do we still have any slots left in our schedule and energy to plan for physical training? Most of us will have a late meal and go to sleep instead… watching the news. Yet, another stress stacking up!

This is where success has led us to. Living in a great neighborhood, driving luxurious cars, and resuming to our task as hamsters running in its wheel, the wheel of stress. That hamster's wheel is not only a daily occupation but a **dynamo** generating most of the stress that we endure and accumulate.

And the next morning, we are back at the office, smiling to welcome our patients, one after the next, absorbing their stresses for a living.

Before the COVID crisis, this would be a pretty accurate portrait of the life of a dentist and of any health private practitioner. Well, COVID did not change that, it amplified each of the stress factors.

Now, the patient present is even more stressed, so it is for us to absorb the extra stress. Now, the financial burden is amplified with all of the cost coming with the lockdown, the lost revenue, the rent or mortgage paid without income, the cost and management of all of the improvised extra protections and changing norms, and the stress of the team members looking to us with most of their own stress.

"COVID rebooted the world. As the systems are restarting,
we now experienced all of its effects simultaneously,
good and bad."
Dr. Bak Nguyen

What we came to accept years ago is now back on the table, all at once. What we deemed natural, COVID shed the light on our choices by default. But deep down, we now realize that we are accepting these conditions and that we must decide to renew our vows as the system is rebooting.

Hosting ALPHA's summits for the last 6 months, I can tell you that I saw and heard the distress within our ranks. Colleagues were coming out, saying that this is too much and not a decent living anymore. Others are addressing the ungratefulness of patients, never recognizing the quality of care offered to them.

Some even walked out from their position, even financially challenged, they preferred to take the time to take care of themselves and to reflect, than to resume a stressful suicidal path.

Some others are busy resuming their practice, upgrading to the new norms, and working days and nights to make up for the lost time. I talked with each and every one of them. It is too obvious to miss. We are playing the **FLIGHT-OR-FIGHT** response to the syllable.

Those dropping out are facing the bull head-on, facing the difficult questions. Those buried in their task resuming, are fleeing as fast as they can to avoid answering those existential questions.

Well, to tell you the truth, after running for a while, the fatigue will catch each of us and we will be facing the same question, at the edge of the cliff, only with more frustration, stress, and less time.

I know this because I faced the bull a few years ago, as I accepted that I chose this profession to honor my parents. I survived my training and dental school only to double down and to open my own clinic months after receiving my licence to practice.

Did I mention that I was turning my back to Hollywood and what could have been a career as a movie producer? More regrets, more doubts, more stress.

Then, after 12 months of operation, as I built one of the modern and refreshing clinics in downtown Montreal, I was facing bankruptcy! Financial burden adding to regrets and doubts. And I found a way to make it through, accepting my choices and leveraging my liabilities, my licence to practice.

"To move ahead, leverage each of your liabilities
so they become assets."
Dr. Bak Nguyen

There are no such things as potential. They are either liabilities or assets. A great possibility that burden you today is a liability, no matter what it can be tomorrow. In the same line of thoughts, an asset that served you well yesterday, but outdated or out of touch, is now your new liability.

That's what I learned facing bankruptcy, doubts and regrets, within the first years of my career. Well, my asset was my creative mind. Now, as a dentist, it was a liability causing me to doubt and to waste much time regretting my choice.

I put that in a box, signing a contract with myself: for the next 10 years, I will apply all of myself being a dentist and putting it all to the service of my patients.

10 years, including that first one spent in hell! Only in 10 years, will I have the luxury to revisit my contract and to look for alternatives and exit strategies.

As a dentist, my liabilities were my clinic, my team, the overhead but also my patients. Each person coming through the door was a possible liability and lawsuit if I did something wrong. I decided to leverage that. I embraced my patients as the salvation I needed to escape my own prison. I was thirsty for genuine connections.

Have you ever put yourself in the shoes of a new patient walking into your office? Well, they feel stressed and know that being there is a necessary evil. They do not want to be there, and neither was I. We connected on that!

My job was to get to know them, connect with them, and try to get them out of my dental chair as soon as possible, taking care of their needs. Needs slowly morphed into desires, fear into trust, and sympathy, into friendship. That's how I escaped bankruptcy, moving on from my regrets and doubts, and embracing my patients.

At that time, I have the fortune to cross path with a gentleman dentist looking to retire, Dr. Roger Bourcier. Even at the edge of a financial cliff, the financing company decided to extend me enough money to buy the practice of Dr. Bourcier.

During the transition time, we became good friends. Roger became my first mentor, showing me that it was possible to be happy as a dentist and to forge genuine friendships from the dental chair. My thirst for human connection and my mentor made me into a human dentist. This is how the tag line of Mdex came to life.

"I am too lazy to spend my life running from something.
I prefer to run towards that something.
It is the shorter way."
Dr. Bak Nguyen

There are no such things as potential. They are either liabilities or assets. A great possibility that burden you today is a liability, no matter what it can be tomorrow. In the same line of thoughts, an asset that served you well yesterday, but outdated or out of touch, is now your new liability.

That's what I learned facing bankruptcy, doubts and regrets, within the first years of my career. Well, my asset was my creative mind. Now, as a dentist, it was a liability causing me to doubt and to waste much time regretting my choice.

I put that in a box, signing a contract with myself: for the next 10 years, I will apply all of myself being a dentist and putting it all to the service of my patients.

10 years, including that first one spent in hell! Only in 10 years, will I have the luxury to revisit my contract and to look for alternatives and exit strategies.

As a dentist, my liabilities were my clinic, my team, the overhead but also my patients. Each person coming through the door was a possible liability and lawsuit if I did something wrong. I decided to leverage that. I embraced my patients as the salvation I needed to escape my own prison. I was thirsty for genuine connections.

Have you ever put yourself in the shoes of a new patient walking into your office? Well, they feel stressed and know that being there is a necessary evil. They do not want to be there, and neither was I. We connected on that!

My job was to get to know them, connect with them, and try to get them out of my dental chair as soon as possible, taking care of their needs. Needs slowly morphed into desires, fear into trust, and sympathy, into friendship. That's how I escaped bankruptcy, moving on from my regrets and doubts, and embracing my patients.

At that time, I have the fortune to cross path with a gentleman dentist looking to retire, Dr. Roger Bourcier. Even at the edge of a financial cliff, the financing company decided to extend me enough money to buy the practice of Dr. Bourcier.

During the transition time, we became good friends. Roger became my first mentor, showing me that it was possible to be happy as a dentist and to forge genuine friendships from the dental chair. My thirst for human connection and my mentor made me into a human dentist. This is how the tag line of **Mdex** came to life.

"For joy, for life."
Dr. Bak Nguyen

Then, I kept seeing more and more patients. I am not friend with all of them, but friendly to each of them. I built from each encounter to meet the people that will help me eventually build the new economic model of dentistry: **Mdex & Co**.

I am not saying this lightly, as the most ambitious project in the dental field ever financed by a bank is **Mdex & Co**. Well, at the finished line, the person who vouched for me and put his head next to mine started as a patient. True story!

I first accepted my fate or choice, but I left the door open ahead, in 10 years. Then, I embraced my liability with an unburden heart, one purged of regrets and doubts. Because I had no expectation and that my heart was emptied, I was available to absorb the stress of my patients. I did not lend them my hands, my skills nor my licence only. I lend them my heart.

Today, against all the odds, I am a success story, as a dentist. That's how I faced the bull right in the eyes. That was 17 years ago. What happened after the 10 years? Well, I missed the mark, being too busy delivering happiness, lending my heart to my patients.

12 years after the opening of my first clinic, after the signature of that contract from me to me, I reopened the door to the possibilities and the alternatives. I was ready to walk out with pride and the satisfaction that I made it as a dentist. But then, a friend, former head of marketing at Telus, made the remark that I was doing great for a dentist who did not dream to become one.

Compared to my peers, I was not showing any signs of depression, fatigue, burnout nor suicidal thoughts. That was odd!

We talked in length that evening. Then I realized that I can simply not erase 12 years of my life. Those 12 years made me who I am, a loved dentist, and now, one that has something to share with his peers.

I got to work and started writing down all the tricks and mental sets that I built to keep myself in check, being a good dentist, one not burden by the ghosts of the past, regrets nor doubts.

That's how I built **Mdex & Co.**, building in infrastructure and philosophy what I wished I could have found while I was facing my life dilemma of following my dreams or honoring my parents with my dental licence.

I built a professional template that allows people to avoid that hard choice. Yes, it is possible to have it all, tweaking the actual formula and mastering the art of prioritizing.

For those of you intrigued with **Mdex & Co.**, I invite you to look up my 7th book, **CHANGING THE WORLD FROM A DENTAL CHAIR**, available on Amazon and Apple Books, but also streaming as a **U.A.X.** (ultimate audio experience) on Spotify and Apple Music. That initiative earned me the nomination of **Ernst and Young Entrepreneur of the year** and **LinkedIn Award and TownHall for Achiever of the year**.

The point here is that I was buried with stress and regrets. I chose to see them as stimuli and to leverage on them.

Standing at the edge of the financial cliff took care of doubts and procrastination.

"The day I emptied my heart of all the burdens,
that day, success, joy, and friendship came to me.
They've been my companions ever since."
Dr. Bak Nguyen

So I faced the bull head-on. Then, I flee being too busy. I still had to face the mirror eventually. I accepted my past and give myself the chance to see the future without compromise, only to understand that my best asset was the experience of the last 12 years doing something I hate, with people I came to love.

The twist was now to help my peers, sharing my secrets and mental sets. In a sense, that was a huge promotion, since I used to make the world a better place, a smile at a time. Now, helping my peers to renew their passion, each of those smiles created by them, will also be part of my ledger! And that is leveraging.

I don't say that I do not feel any stress today, but it is a signal, not a storm. COVID put that philosophy to the test, heavily. I was stressed again, but as I resumed clinical duty, I had to empty my heart in order to lend it to my patients. That took care of the stress for a while.

And then, more financial challenges and confinement issues got stress to resurface. Well, I made my peace with it, knowing that I am not the cause of that stress and that no matter how much I could outperform, the stress will be imposed.

Since I do not expect stress to go away, I feel better already. The only thing that I can do is to apply myself to make sure that my patients feel safe under my care, even in COVID times.

From that success, I am leveraging the needed inspiration to keep moving forward. With my Alpha peers, we look into our problems, of how to cope with stress as a profession. Many ideas are appearing. Some might lead to concrete measures, some will be a good topic for a Summit.

We are open and sharing. This is how Ken and I came together and as a result, you are riding this journey with us. In a word, I started by listing the kinds of stress we are submitting ourselves to daily.

And then, overwhelmed, we try to flee until we arrive at the edge of the cliff. I told you my story and how I made it out alive and grew from the journey.

If competition was once and asset pushing us through dental and medical school, pushing us through Life, well, that asset has grown to become one of the biggest liability today, as we lost the capability to connect genuinely. The trust and connection with a mentor will take care of that.

Empty your heart and lend it to your patient. Open your heart and welcome the help of a mentor, in short keep your heart light. Your past medals are your new burdens.

This is just as true as your past mistake can be your next opportunity. Learn to empty your heart to gain clarity, the clarity to see a liability from and asset.

"Hope is not something to be found, but something to be heard. Hope is that little voice inside of our heart as we wake up every morning."
Dr. Bak Nguyen

This is **TOUCHSTONE**, leveraging today's psychological smog.

STRESS is part of life, for better and for worse.
Better since it can be leveraged
Worse, if it is in control
Dr. BAK NGUYEN

CHAPTER 4

ANTI-SOCIAL MEDIA

by Dr. KEN SEROTA

"It is imperative that the internal monologue
brought about by social media is muted."
Dr. Ken Serota

Social media contributes much to the quality and substance of our lives. It is a powerful motivator, it builds community, introduces us to mentors or influencers, teaches us to develop our own unique voice, and expands our communication skills and technological creativity.

However, it can be responsible for **loneliness** and **depression**, can create a sense of "missing out" on social events, the latest trends, and deny us the achievement of personal goals which could be seen as less than.

Envy and shame by feeling a state of comparison are both illogical and fraught with a lack of perspective. Regardless, the impact can be damaging.

The images and comments shared by friends, colleagues, and strangers reflect a **biased perspective** from the contributor. Many people's social feeds only highlight the positive moments of their life, making it seem like they don't have the same challenging or mundane experiences as the rest of us.

It's highly unlikely that negative experiences or disappointments will be shared. Instead, we are forced to compare ourselves to idealized messages and photos of our friends, peers, and celebrities.

Activity online is an activity not in the moment, we are not mindful of our surroundings. The number of hours spent online leads to a state of distraction, interrupted focus, disruption in the quantity and quality of our sleep, which is crucial to healthy development and well-being. In extreme cases, cyberbullying and online harassment have led to suicide.

This is not to dismiss the value of social media engagement. The responsible use of social media tools can help quickly disseminate important new information, relevant new scientific findings, share diagnostic, treatment, and follow-up protocols, as well as compare different approaches used globally, removing geographic boundaries for the first time in our history.

In the case of the COVID-19 pandemic, health organizations have worked assiduously to mitigate the attendant mental health issues by advocacy through dental associations using social media.

Informational, emotional and peer support, and health behavior change are at the vanguard of controlling the psychological stress resulting from fear of contagion and the social isolation of lockdown.

"Social media brings an immediacy to this communication as it offers a voice, not an email."
Dr. Ken Serota

Regardless of the disembodiment, it has a personal connotation. At an individual level, a panic response to COVID with no vaccine insight could be psychologically perilous to mental health.

In the face of medical uncertainty, people rely heavily on social media for accessing health information in their own social media groups. It makes evolutionary sense for people to develop a strong sense of sharing health.

While excessive use of social media content during a public health crisis could be rewarding, it can also take a toll on mental health.

There is no easy fix to people's stress disorders during a pandemic. Some may choose ordinary coping methods they used before to deal with new stressors, while others try to reinforce a strong sense of resilience.

Still, others choose damaging and dangerous means, also representative of the radical uncontrolled impact of social media. It is a herd mentality of destructive proportions.

It was presumed that politics played a key role in distracting people from considering accuracy on social media. In fact, the intuitive or emotional thinking that has led to the assimilation of misinformation relates more to superstition or the pervasive attempt to see matters through the lens of conspiracies as espoused by real or supposedly fake news.

This can be cataclysmic as social media content is invariably seen as truth due to the incessant fusillade of posting and reposting.

It is virtually impossible to distance oneself from social media, however, there is recourse to the negative impact of social media.

Instagram and Twitter offer mute features that will stop posts from specific organizations or individuals from appearing in your feed. You can also unfollow someone on Facebook, while still remaining Facebook friends with them.

Twitter provides a mute option for keywords or hashtags that trigger or upset the reader. With this feature, you can mute them forever or just for a limited time, which can be great if you need a break from content that is a heavy burden for you, such as the news.

COVID demands that we respond more aggressively recreating positivity on social media. Too often we are use artifice such as filters and Photoshop to create an unauthentic self. COVID is not aware of artifice and addressing it with a skewed perspective only adds to the stress when reality intervenes.

To mitigate social media stress exacerbated by COVID, it is advisable to; cut social media use by setting blocks of time aside to disconnect, charge devices in a dedicated room, not in a bedroom, turn notifications will reduce your impulse to check your phone or device every time it alerts you and remove social media apps from your phone, making it harder for you to easily check your accounts.

By limiting social media usage to a tablet or computer, you should be able to decrease your social media use drastically. Perhaps the greatest drawback to social media is its' otherworldliness.

The vast majority of us play, not learn, during our online time. Dense text and more esoteric topics do not engage the way that same way as emojis and .gifs.

Real-time information sharing system of important COVID related health data is readily supplanted by the jargon of misinformation and disinformation. They are couched in pop culture terms, therefore more readily digested.

Trust comes from memes, jingoistic terms, humor, satire and in the worst possible example of cruelty. We cannot turn our eyes away no matter how unpleasant.

The acute stress caused by this exposure can also result in a positive feedback loop, whereby those who are most concerned will tend to seek out COVID-19 related content more readily.

The algorithmic structure of social media programming will further exacerbate this, as a pursuit of Covid-19 related links will result in the software proposing further links of a similar topic, leading to confirmation bias and distortion of risk perception.

Health anxiety precipitated by media over-exposure can cause unnecessary distress and can result in help-seeking behavior which may be **disproportionate** to actual need.

"We are damned with social media, we are damned without it. It is a tool, not a magic bullet."
Dr. Ken Serota

We are not as yet protected from misinformation or disinformation by oversight at the highest level. It will come or social media could be the most damaging force in our future. It is the fear that manifests with artificial intelligence.

We are, however, not without recourse, there is an OFF button or switch which should be used with **extreme prejudice** when called for.

This is **TOUCHSTONE**, leveraging today's psychological smog.

STRESS is part of life, for better and for worse.
Better since it can be leveraged
Worse, if it is in control
Dr. BAK NGUYEN

CHAPTER 5

PSYCHOLOGICAL SMOG

by Dr. BAK NGUYEN

This is the heart of this book, this project, **Psychological Smog**. This is what Ken wanted his work and this book to be about. I must say that even if I liked the imagery of the **Psychological Smog**, I couldn't see clearly the narrative in play. 2 interviews later, he brought me to his view.

"Nature has designed STRESS as a stimulus.
We, we have made it our by default response
to the stimulus itself."
Dr. Bak Nguyen

And that is why it is so hard to treat or to relieve stress today. It is simply everywhere. From being late to work, being stuck in traffic to who to date and how we look on social media. If Life was a competition, well, we took the concept to the next level, constantly submitting ourselves to more and more pressure.

"I say pressure because most of us
are reacting, not pro acting."
Dr. Bak Nguyen

From expectations to standards to rules, the walls are closing down on us and the pressure keeps raising. From the lies of perfection to the fear of failure, both society and ourselves are to blame to keep cranking up the pressure. The steam resulting is that **Psychological Smog** that Ken is talking about.

That **Smog** is, in itself, a new source of stress. Well, to be blunt, that **Smog** is not from yesterday. Since our childhood, that is what we know and came to accept as normal.

The **walls closing** on us are our education, societal behaviors, and good manners, they are the rules and the laws we live by. Those were the first set of walls, those were the boundaries of living together. Thank God those walls were there.

The problem came next. As the strategy is proven efficient, that concept of domestication got picked up by more and more people to add more and more walls within the confinement of the boundaries of society. Education and training were the champions of raising the temperature and the pressure.

The consumption industries took care of the rest, showing us who we can be, what we can eat, where we can sleep. If we stopped for an instance and have an honest look at our lives, we are living the scene of a magazine from our childhood.

Is that an Instyle magazine, is that a Playboy magazine, is that Forbes, Times, or the IKEA catalog? It does not matter, we are living in one or more of these constructs, looking for our happiness and our identity.

That was true before, but now, at the social media age, it became irrefutable. 5 minutes on Instagram, Facebook, and LinkedIn will tell you in what magazine you are living your life, your projected life.

We all do it. I, myself, lived the projections of my parent for nearly 35 years, and it is still a part of me. Is that a problem? Well, it depends on how you are taking in the inputs.

Are all of these magazines and standards more perfection for you to obtain, or are there stepping stones and templates for you to break free and to find your own reality?

The **Stress of the Smog** is mainly due to the fact that we do not see the Smog as abnormal. Bathing in that Smog for so long, all that we do is to react to the Smog we see, not differentiating the boundaries from the expectations, the alternatives from the distractions.

What we do is simply to replace one element of the Smog for another, constantly. You don't believe me? Close your eyes and visualize what is on your mind right now. Name the 3 first words that came to your mind.

Those may be sources of anxiety, fear or obligation you have to face. Then, let's imagine that I took all of those 3 away. How free do you feel? Do you feel the liberation of the emptiness, the black emptiness of nothing?

As soon as the **Psychological Smog** is cleared, you are replacing it right away with a new **Smog**, even a thicker one. We all do. It is a little like we are afraid of looking at the emptiness.

"Emptiness is not a void, but the absence of worries, of interests. Somehow, we came to fear that emptiness as a void of life."
Dr. Bak Nguyen

We can debate this as much as you want, but that **Smog** is the primary air that you are breathing day in and day out. We are all intoxicated by our own Smog.

If the **Smog** isn't too dense, it is a normal day. Is the **Smog** is getting more intense and morphing into **Fog**, that impairs our vision, then, we call for help. The problem is that the **Fog** wasn't new, it came from our tolerance to **Smog**. Only, this time, we had the clarity of mind to detect the smoke clouding our perception of reality.

On one side you have the Smog, menacing anytime to become a Fog, on the other, the walls are closing down, always asking you to be more, to be perfect, to keep pushing, grinding… How do we break that cycle?

Well, this is a book and a journey. We are merely at chapter 5 of 14. I should just keep painting you the Smog and how deep we are within our problems, but that is not my style. I hate to lose my time, so I won't waste yours.

By now, you know my story. Expectation, stress, education, religion, my Smog was thick the day I was born, the immigrant status of my parents made sure of that. To be born with the expectation that your name isn't complete until you can put a Dr. in front of it, isn't a sane way to build confidence.

I paid my dues and got in dental school. You know the rest of the story. But beyond that Smog and social pressure, I had my own aspirations and dreams as an artist and a sensitive soul. That Smog was cutting on my influx of air. I tried to fight it, but it was hopeless.

Imagine a young immigrant boy of 10 telling his parents that Life isn't what they are living in! Even worse, try telling them that there is more to life than that reality! You are in for a long night. That reminds me of Russell Peter sketches… it sounds funny, but that's a reality, pure reality.

I learned from a young age that the only way for me to have my time and air, was to give them what they wanted first, but not telling them that I was done, so they wouldn't burden me with even more on my plate.

At school, I was often amongst the first to finish my homework and to go home without my backpack. That worked like a charm until I reach dental school. Then, the pressure was simply too great to use the same stratagem. So I reversed the elements.

Studying seems never to be enough and there was always more to read, more to learn and blablabla... So I paid myself first, to borrow from Robert Kiyosaki. I have fun first, and then, as the dates of the exams were closing down on me, I studied the essential within the nights and hours before the crucial moment.

I will not recommend this strategy for the fainted hearts, it has its toll on your soul. But to me, it was working. This is how I graduated Dental school, not with honors, but with record, being the first student to even produced an independent movie while attending dental school.

This is how the doors of Hollywood were, at some point, open to me. But that is another story.

The idea here is that I refused the Pressure. I hated the Pressure! So I changed it into Tension. That thickness of the Smog suffocating me, was so thick that I could stand on it, so I did. I used it as stepping stones and suddenly, I had clarity, I was free for a moment.

Then, in dental school, I was finding my voice and had the time of my life discovering my sensitive soul, making movies. That wasn't Smog, it was magic.

I took that clarity and positive vibe back to my medical studies. Now, I was facing a choice, why do I keep putting up with the Smog and the Pressure? Because fighting it will be even harder.

To eliminate the possibility of those existential questions that could suck me into a never-ending void, I raised the pressure to the maximal level, giving me very little time to learn the requirement of dental medicine.

"I dictate my own terms. That's how I transpose Pressure into Tension."
Dr. Bak Nguyen

In business, there is that saying that there are two parts to every deal: the **price** and the **terms**. Both the price and the terms are important, and playing between them will either make it the best of deals or the worse of deals.

I was paying the price anyway, having to excel at school, and eventually, to graduate. If that was the price, I stretched the terms to its maximum. It is then that I learned that those walls surrounding us were very easy to push and to get rid of.

I am not talking about breaking the laws of society. There are so many inner layers of walls to push and to clean before I had to face those boundaries of society.

Most of my inner walls, I struck down. But then, just like any of you, new walls appeared faster than I could break them. I refused to let go and I kept pushing. I became a master breaking down the walls, only to realize that the better I get good at it, the thicker and the higher the walls were becoming.

This is one of the primal laws of the Universe, action-reaction. The day I understood that, that day I found peace for a moment. It was pure wisdom.

So what to do? Well, I had a stratagem that was working perfectly well back in elementary and high school: to use the walls as stepping stones. Before it was Smog, thick smog but still Smog.

Now that I destroyed so many walls so many times, those forming my Smogs were made of brick and concrete. Stepping on them was almost not a metaphor. This is how I elevated myself to clarity, giving up the inner fighting and not fleeing, but embracing them instead.

I do it and I got rid of the task as soon as possible to free my horizon of the Smog, for a moment. This is how I became a loved and good dentist, getting rid of the fear and replacing it with trust and friendship. This is how I saved millions in marketing and became a motivational speaker.

It is also the key to my superpower writing books, waking up 2 hours before dawn to have clarity and the opportunity to talk with my sub-conscience.

The **Psychological Smog** is a reality of our modern society. We each bathed in our *original mix*. You can't fight it. You can't run from it, since it is part of your desire and identity. Learn to see it for what it is and step on it. Leverage it so you can elevate yourself to clarity and for a moment of freedom, perhaps even happiness.

And how do you leverage your Smog? Well, start dictating your terms instead of submitting to them. You are paying the full price anyway! Having your terms, you can either make sure that you can afford that price or make up for that price in half of the time. This is what I meant by being lazy.

Forget perfection, look to deliver and to learn. This is all you can and should ask of yourself. Look beyond that **Smog** and since you know your **Smog** inside and out, you are in the best position to leverage it, knowing its triggers and weak spots.

Is this a good way to relieve the stress from your system? Well, stress is a stimulus, remember?

Now that you are in control of your system, that you dictate the term, you do not want the stimuli to stop. On the contrary, those are helping you to achieve your goals.

This is **TOUCHSTONE**, leveraging today's psychological smog.

STRESS is part of life, for better and for worse.
Better since it can be leveraged
Worse, if it is in control
Dr. BAK NGUYEN

84

CHAPTER 6

TECHNOLOGY AND MENTAL HEALTH

by Dr. KEN SEROTA

Change in health care delivery is being driven by the widespread availability of "digital technology". Computers, the internet, mobile devices such as smartphones, and mobile software applications are effective tools, but they must be used judiciously and with effect by the providers.

The use of digital interventional practices will have a considerable impact on clinical practice and treatment. The paradigm shift will, however, require an acute paradigm shift as it is antithetical in the extreme to traditional and historic modes.

Technology has opened a new frontier in mental health support and data collection. Mobile devices like cell phones, smartphones, and tablets are giving the public, doctors, and researchers new ways to access help, monitor progress, and increase understanding of well being.

Society has embraced digital technology in the home, at work, for pleasure, for learning. As such, the paradigm shift will not be as egregious for the young who are manifesting mental issues at an alarming rate.

Anyone with the ability to send a text message can contact a crisis center. New technology can also be packaged into extremely sophisticated apps for smartphones or tablets. Such apps might use the device's built-in sensors to collect information on a user's typical behavior patterns.

If the app detects a change in behavior, it may provide a signal that help is needed before a crisis occurs. There are stand-alone apps that show promise to improve memory or thinking skills.

Others help the user connect to a peer counsellor or to a health care professional. The power of connection brings an immediacy to the danger of mental issues, in essence "you are never truly alone".

"Help is simply a learned muscle movement."
Dr. Ken Serota

This new era of mental health technology offers great opportunities but also raises a number of concerns. Tackling potential problems will be an important part of making sure new apps provide benefits without causing harm.

That is why the mental health community and software developers are focusing on:

1. **effectiveness**; the biggest concern with technological interventions is obtaining scientific evidence that they work and that they work as well as traditional methods.

2. **for whom and for what**; another concern is understanding if apps work for all people and for all mental health conditions.

3. **privacy**; apps deal with very sensitive personal information so app makers need to be able to guarantee privacy for app users.

4. **guidance**; There are no industry-wide standards to help consumers know if an app or other mobile technology is proven effective.

5. **regulation**; the question of who will or should regulate mental health technology and the data it generates needs to be answered, and overselling. There is some concern that if an app or program promises more than it delivers, consumers may turn away from other, more effective therapies.

Digital technology opens up new modes of assessment. Virtual reality procedures can assess sensitivity to particular environments and the presence of sensors in smartphones makes it possible to track many phenomena on an ongoing basis including sleep, movement, physical activity, speech, device usage, and the person's location).

How to use this information is only just beginning to be explored. It may prove possible to catch new episodes at a very early stage and supply interventions at the very time that users might benefit most "Real-time" intervention might be especially relevant to suicide prevention if markers of imminent risk could be identified.

However, psychopathology tracking is not necessarily benign. It can magnify rumination and self-focus, and it has been reported to trigger emotional instability. Similarly, the immediate delivery of interventions might create reliance upon them which could interfere with the acquisition of self-management skills.

The immediate focus should be on reducing barriers to using digital mental health to extend existing services. However, digital technologies can also be harnessed to simultaneously provide preventive, well–being, self–management, and clinical interventions to populations at scale, to implement stepped–care models, and to provide paraprofessional or even automated support via technology such as chatbots. These functions are rarely addressed in current mental health delivery systems.

Thus, in addition to harnessing digital technology for more traditional functions, longer–term goals should include introducing truly innovative digital mental health practices into the health care system.

COVID has highlighted the great need for digital mental health interventions, but also the barriers to their Global collaborative models be pivotal for yielding the systems and policy–level changes needed.

Indeed, now is the time to catalyze change and comprehensively address the barriers that have prevented widespread delivery of health services to the millions of people who would benefit.

This is **TOUCHSTONE**, leveraging today's psychological smog.

STRESS is part of life, for better and for worse.
Better since it can be leveraged
Worse, if it is in control

CHAPTER 7

TOUCHSTONES

by Dr. BAK NGUYEN

And so we are back to the title of this book. What are the touchstones, the triggers to our stress? As we covered that in the last chapter, our habits and training got us to grow into and from a permanent **PSYCHOLOGICAL SMOG**.

I personally do not believe that to get rid of that **SMOG** is possible since we will be replacing ourselves, one stress for another as soon as one is dealt with.

I personally do not believe that to get rid of that **SMOG** is possible since we will be replacing ourselves, that stimulus with another as soon as one is dealt with.

The repetition was just to prove my point. No one wants the stress and we tend to stay away from stress as much as possible. But stimulus? Well, what started as a fun stimulus will eventually lose its charm and turn into a todo, then a burden or a failed promise. Déjà vu?

So no, I do not believe that getting rid of the **SMOG** is possible, at least not for our generation. To start to understand stress for what it is, a *stimulus informing us of a change* is a start.

To not attach emotions that would amplify and distort that stimulus will be the challenge. Pain is a signal and a message. The fear of pain is a **SMOG** lasting much longer than the pain itself and causing much more mental damage due to apprehension.

So where is the stress, is it the pain or the fear of the pain? Fear, that's a master touchstone, one that we all carry around. Can one confront his or her pain and be free from it?

Yes, but to do so, you will have to **walk through fire** to be cleansed. I've been there and I can tell you that it is not a way of living. The trauma of the process far exceeds its benefits and… eventually, its effects fade away.

"Nothing drilled in by an exterior force will last forever. Nature has its ways to resume its course. It is called time."
Dr. Bak Nguyen

If you ask me, we should identify our **Fears**, try to understand them. Not to rationalize them, but to understand why and how, and accept them for what they are. It is bad enough to fear, no one needs to fear **FEAR** on top of that!

I have my fears. I know where they lay and I do not hide from them. Acknowledging them, day in and day out, they become facts and furniture of my psychic. With the light shed on them, they lost much of the **theatric effect** of *dramatization* and they become just another stimulus, not **THE** red button on the **FOOTBALL**.

Is this the best way to confront our fears? That's the best way that I found and it works for me. But the only way that it can work is as you decided to do so by your own will.

If someone is forcing you, even convincing you to live with your fears and to have them out in the light of your comfort zone, it will be a trauma and the side effects will largely out weight the benefit.

The only way to deal with your fears is to know the way and to deal with them on your pace, your terms, and your timing. The smallest details off will throw you years back. I am talking from experience.

To talk about your fears is another way. In my experience, every time you do that, you are giving more importance to something that already taking more weight than it should. I am not sure of the logic of the process. But it is still better than to run from your fears than to convince yourself that they do not exist.

Fear, just like **PSYCHOLOGICAL SMOG**, when hidden away and locked into a box, will keep growing and raising the pressure. I prefer to avoid that kind of steam, so my fears are laying around as plants in a corner. They are just part of the decor.

I learned very quickly that to share your fears openly, even in a safe environment, is a dangerous game. You never know who is listening and who will use those against you. So I do not talk about my fears. I do not hide them or run from them either. They are simply lying around in the corner.

Forty years plus and you know what? I threw some of those fears away, by mistake, while I was cleaning around. Figuratively speaking, of course. How do I know that? Writing, I have the chance to relive the events and the emotions.

Well, some of my fears back then are now nowhere to be found. Writing about the events, I can clearly feel the grip that that fear had on me back then. And you know what? Looking back, I do not feel much. No anger, no bitter taste, just a fact that I was afraid then, and I am not anymore. This is what I wish for all of you.

Some people believe that fear is what's keeping us in line and it acts as a survival safeguard. I can tell you that I am pretty aware of the danger when there is one, my stress is still working in that sense. The only difference is that I receive the signal as an entry, and not before the change is occurring. Before, fear would haunt me much before the actual danger occurs. Was that a safe way to prepare?

Well, I must say that it was an inefficient way since fearful, I was handicapped and did not have full access to my complete capabilities. Not the best odds of survival!

On the contrary, because I used my **SMOG** as a stepping stone today, I can see clearly the horizon. And trust me, with **clarity**, you can see the change coming from miles away. Prepare for that change and readjust on the way. That's the only real good advice I can give you, from experience.

Other than **FEAR**, what would be the second touchstone? **PLEASE TO BELONG** will come next if you ask me. Trying to please someone else and sacrificing your own opinions and preference to please another part will come next on the list.

Can we get rid of that one? I would say, of course, just don't mind what people think of you. Much harder to do than to say! If you studied the pyramid of Maslow about the psychology of motivation and needs, the first layers were about survival and reproduction.

By the third layer, it is about a sense of belonging. What is surprising is that the sense of belonging comes before the need for self-esteem. What does that tell you?

That the **stress of belonging** and of pleasing is a natural need. So the stress coming with it is not one that will disappear anytime soon. To do things that you do not want to please others isn't an exception but rather a norm.

How to fix that? Well, within my forty-some years of experience, I spent more than half of my life pleasing others, my parents in particular. Then, I had to fit in the mold of being a doctor when I was a sensitive soul and an artist. I must say that it wasn't easy and a painful process.

SELF-ACTUALIZATION

ESTEEM

LOVE/BELONGING

SAFETY

PHYSIOLOGICAL NEEDS

THE PYRAMID OF ABRAHAM MASLOW

But then, as I found true love, my sense of belonging was not as high anymore and self-esteem took over. The magic happened when my confidence was strong enough to detach myself from the need of belonging.

I always thought that the Pyramid was hierarchic, but it is not. I could build on the top layers even if I got rid of the last one. Some will argue that love replaced my need of belonging, I can't argue with that. The point I wanted to make here was how to not trigger the touchstone of **PLEASING OTHERS**, well, find love, and build your confidence.

The first transformation that one will notice, transitioning from insecure to confident, is morphing from a wannabe to be. From there, being authentic will take all of its significance.

On that note, the love I shared with my wife and best friend, Tranie Vo changed the game for me. But later on, the love I discover being a father got me to the next level. Today, I please because I am kind and generous, not because I care.

The difference is that I still give, but the reaction of the other party does not affect me anymore. If the other party is grateful, I am happy. If the other party is ungrateful, well, that is none of my concern. The loss isn't mine.

Becoming a father, I found purpose and my place in life. That overwrote all of my insecurities and doubts. I also noticed that it straighten my needs and desires as described in the Pyramid of Maslow. In a word, it sorted out all the shoulds from the musts.

Becoming a dad, I had to be the man I wanted my son to become so he has a model to copy. That worked like a charm since to him, the was no pressure, just tension, and inspiration. At 7 years old, my son wanted to write books with me. At 8, he co-authored 22 books with his dad!

I am covering this subject to reinforce the notion of confidence. I became confident because my wife loved me and believed in me. Then that confidence grew stronger as I became a dad, I found my purpose in life. I must tell you that most of my fears took care of themselves.

*"The day I became a father, most of my fears faded away.
I had too much to do to be fearful."*
Dr. Bak Nguyen

The third touchstone is **FAILURE**. To fail is a burden in our society, especially to highly trained professionals. Well, that's the way we were raised. To fail is a stress in itself since it set our esteem back.

The stress is then amplified by having to face the judgment of others, often laughing at our failure. Our sense of belonging is then crushed. Funny thing, notice that those who will laugh the loudest or those having nothing to show... they never failed, they just failed to try something, anything... Just an observation.

So these two stresses are adding up to the fact that we failed and have to face the consequences x3:

- **The failure itself**
- **The self-Esteem**
- **The judgment**

The touchstone of failure may come in third on this list, but its burden over one's soul is as heavy or even heavier than **FEAR**.

This is why most people are so afraid of failing. Read that last part again, being afraid of failing.

FEAR and **FAILURE** are in themselves stressful enough, what happens when you combine them together? And you have now a better image of how the **PSYCHOLOGICAL SMOG** is forming, growing, and getting thicker and thicker.

"Speed is the answer to avoid the touchstone of FAILURE."
Dr. Bak Nguyen

Common wisdom will tell you that you haven't failed if you haven't given up yet; that you haven't failed if you learned something. So to fix failure, one has to get back in the game as soon as possible, smarter.

When you look at the amplifications of the stress of **FAILURE**, **ESTEEM**, and **SOCIAL JUDGMENT**, well those work with time. The more time you have on your hand to think about your failure, the more your **ESTEEM** will be tested. The longer you are sitting on that failure, the more chance you have to meet with people that will judge you.

So your answer is ahead, there is nothing back there for you. Sleep well, eat well, and get back on the action as fast as possible and try again. The cautious people will bench themselves for a while until they figure out what they did wrong.

On paper, that's is a sounded concept. In reality, they will be exposing themselves to 3 times the stress, **FAILURE**, **ESTEEM**, and **JUDGMENT**. The longer the time out, the greater the stress.

You don't believe me? What happens when you get out of a test that you might have missed? Well, what was impossible for you to solve in the exam room, within the next hours will hit you like a brick! This is how we learned. We all do.

Would that be great to have the chance to get back to that specific question and to complete our answer? Well, guess what? In real life, we often have that chance to do so. But how many of us will take that opportunity?

"Second chances are no myths, they are real.
But the window of opportunity is right after the failure.
The longer we wait, the narrower the window gets."
Dr. Bak Nguyen

This is why I am saying that **SPEED** is the essence that will help you avoid the stress coming with the third touchstone, **FAILURE**. React to your mistake, and get back in the game as everything is still clear, as the condition hasn't changed that much, and as

TIME did not yet has the chance to chip neither your **ESTEEM** nor your sense of **BELONGING**.

I wrote 72 books within 36 months. I wrote my first one within 2 weeks. Well, I remembered that the experts I was consulting to have it published were not pleased to talk about the 2 weeks period. To them, it sounds pretentious and took away the prestige of writing a book itself.

Since I was new to the game, I followed their advice. Three months later, many publishing companies rejected the manuscript. The rejection was hard on my morale, my **TOUCHSTONE of FAILURE** was red.

Within these three months, I also received many, many comments from my surroundings telling me how to write books and tell me what to improve in my writing, even how my writing was odd. I listened to everyone.

That's on one side. On the other, I kept walking up 2 hours earlier every morning, without any alarm, and had time to kill. I resume writing within 2 weeks. By the time the rejections arrived, I was on my 5th book.

The rejections were hard. My self-esteem was safe from chipping since I was now way ahead in terms of production, I was starting my speaking career and started to get recognition as a world record author.

About the judgment, well, there were there, but before I could give them any attention, most of the opinions were obsolete anyway. **SPEED** changed everything.

Amongst the first criticisms that I received, some were saying that I was looking for my 5 minutes of fame, self-promoting. By the 5th book, I was a genius serial author, not any kind of wannabe looking for attention anymore. I never heard from these people again.

And guess what? I was doing the exact same thing, waking up earlier in the morning to have a private time with my sub-conscience and to put my thought into words.

I also got better with words, mastering English, which isn't my primary tongue, mastering more and more the art of narration, and developing a skill to share complex philosophical concepts or financial concepts, but in everyday words. I developed my own style and narrative.

72 books later, you are sharing my journey. And **SPEED**? It eased most of the edges and challenges I encountered on the way. I did and got it out. I learned and got better, producing more, faster, bolder, and bigger. I scored world record after world record.

And the **TOUCHSTONES**? Well, the first three publishers never published my books. But today, **BARNES and NOBLES** are distributing them.

This is **TOUCHSTONE**, leveraging today's psychological smog.

STRESS is part of life, for better and for worse.
Better since it can be leveraged
Worse, if it is in control
Dr. BAK NGUYEN

CHAPTER 8

TELEDENTISTRY

by Dr. KEN SEROTA

Teledentistry is an impacting modality for patient care at a distance, using information and communication technologies (e.g., "virtual visits") offering services to patients in different physical locations.

The inability to see patients during the COVID lockdown was precipitous. Lack of face-to-face communication led to patient apprehension regarding the proper communication of their problems to their dentists. This paradigm shift will take time to recalibrate.

COVID made it risky for patients to physically enter dental practices for treatment other than emergency care. It is the natural extension of marketing tool connectivity done for patient retention, advisories of health innovations, and new technologies available in the practitioner's facility.

It is the dynamic versus static connection that begun with websites and e-mail blasts. Digital outreach began years prior to COVID, but COVID as in so many things manifested as a catalyst for the immediacy of response in so many areas.

There are two categories of **TELEDENTISTRY**:

Synchronous teledentistry uses real-time interaction between patient and provider utilizing a data or video conferencing tool, and/or audiovisual telecommunications technology. Patient communication is traditionally synchronous and linear and yet, the introduction of virtual and augmented reality, possibly haptics and in time holography will change this approach dramatically.

Asynchronous teledentistry involves the transmission of recorded health information (e.g., radiographs, photographs, video, digital impressions, and photomicrographs of patients) through a secure electronic communications system to a practitioner, who uses the information to evaluate a patient's condition or render a service outside of a real-time or live interaction.

Remote patient monitoring (RPM): Personal health and medical data collection from an individual in one location via electronic communication technologies, which is transmitted to a provider (sometimes via a data processing service) in a different location for use in care and related support of care.

Mobile health (mHealth): Health care and public health practice and education supported by mobile communication devices, such as cell phones, tablet computers, and personal digital assistants (PDA).

Teledentistry can be provided in a number of ways, including, as examples: Live video (synchronous): Live, two-way interaction between a person (patient, caregiver, or provider) and a provider. Store-and-forward (asynchronous).

Teledentistry is not a replacement for physical dental examinations. However, dentists have found effective ways to utilize this technology to treat their patients. Some use cases we found include emergency patient evaluation, orthodontic consultations, oral health education, and remote care in nursing homes.

During COVID-19, teledentistry has proven itself to be a valuable tool for dentists to evaluate urgent patients and measure the severity of their condition.

It is easier for dentists to assess patients with face-to-face conversations using video conferencing tools, rather than communicating with patients over the phone. For example, patients can actually show dentists their chipped tooth or gum abscesses in a video chat.

Many factors can inhibit senior citizens from visiting the dentist's office, including mobility issues or compromised immune systems. Teledentistry allows dentists to treat senior citizens remotely, circumventing these barriers.

The Foundation For Post-Acute and Long-Term Care Medicine conducted a study to evaluate the accuracy of teledentistry for diagnosing dental pathology, assessing the rehabilitation status of dental prostheses, and evaluating the chewing ability of older adults living in nursing homes.

The study found that teledentistry showed excellent accuracy for diagnosing dental pathology in older adults living in nursing homes, and its use may allow more regular checkups to be carried out by dental professionals.

A lesser-known use case for teledentistry is conducting oral health classes with patients. I spoke to several dentists who have utilized video conferencing tools to offer smoking cessation counselling or proper oral care classes for kids. This is a great way to remain engaged with your patients while dental practices are shut down.

Teledentistry provides several benefits including increased safety, added revenue, and increased access to care in rural areas.

Shelter-in-place orders and mandatory shutdowns have had a negative impact on dental practices nationwide. Offering virtual appointments is one way you can continue to make your practice money despite these restrictions.

Teledentistry allows dentists and patients to connect regardless of their physical location. This could be particularly valuable to a country like Canada, with a population of nearly 38 million citizens distributed across a vast geographic area.

According to the University of Western Ontario Medical Journal, Canada's widespread geography has created an urban concentration of medical care and left most rural areas severely underserved.

Teledentistry could be a useful tool to help citizens of less-populated and underdeveloped regions access oral health services. It could potentially make treatment more cost-effective and accessible by lowering costs by reducing the need to travel.

The possibility of virtually bringing specialists and general providers into remote areas is important for patients living there who have limited access to care.

Someone in a rural setting, for example, would no longer need to make a trip to receive an initial diagnosis or in some cases to return for follow-up if they could discuss this virtually with their dentist and send an image over the internet.

For a dental practice, remote consultation may not be noticeably more cost-effective than ordinary in-person care. For the patient, however, eliminating the need to travel or take as much time off from work could greatly reduce costs.

A study of residential aged care facilities, published by the Journal of Telemedicine and Telecare, suggests the cost of remote appointments is lower than or equivalent to current standards when asynchronous teledentistry is provided.

However, in this analysis, synchronous teledentistry was slightly more expensive than face-to-face treatment. The researchers acknowledge that the appropriate situations for remote appointments and in-person care may differ.

The lack of acceptance of teledentistry by the dentists can be attributed to the fact that they may find it complex and may be resistant to new skills. They may be technologically challenged, be afraid of making an inaccurate diagnosis, and be concerned about increased costs and expenses.

There may be constraints related to infrastructure, such as, poor internet access, shortage of hardware, lack of training, lack of technical support, and expertise.

There are efficacy and accuracy concerns. Two-dimensional representation of lesions and inability to perform tests like palpation and auscultation are other limitations. To overcome these challenges, dentists must be trained adequately and educated about this technology, which will increase the acceptance of teledentistry.

The need of the hour is to incorporate teledentistry into routine dental practice. It will not replace traditional modes of treatment, it will at least complement the existing **compromised dental system** during the current pandemic and future contagions. Its use post-pandemic may be in question, however, cost containment, reduction in lost time, and income for patients among numerous other factors will most certainly ensure that it will occupy an ongoing role of great importance.

This is **TOUCHSTONE**, leveraging today's psychological smog.

STRESS is part of life, for better and for worse.
Better since it can be leveraged
Worse, if it is in control
Dr. BAK NGUYEN

CHAPTER 9

MIRAGES

by Dr. BAK NGUYEN

I could have titled this chapter Touchstone part 2, but I really believed that I covered the hard touchstones already: **FEAR**, **BELONGING**, and **FAILURE**.

In this chapter, I would like to cover with you the other touchstones. Contrary to the hard touchstones which you have to learn to live with until they fade away by themselves, the **MIRAGES** or soft touchstones are from a different nature. Those, the right mindset can erase and put aside.

There are **4 MIRAGES TOUCHSTONES**:
- **DOUBTS**
- **PERFECTION**
- **DENIAL**
- **PROCRASTINATION**

"Touchstones are triggers of the stress hormonal reaction. Knowing your way around them will shape your personality."
Dr. Bak Nguyen

That's a pretty bold statement, and one you will be shaped by, even if you disagree with the affirmation. In the stock market, it is well known that people are motivated either by **FEAR** or by **GREED**. Knowing what emotions a trader is fuelling on will indicate his behaviors and following trades.

In the same line of thoughts, those touchstones releasing stress, we discover them, we experience them, we try to keep them safe and away. Well, that determines our personality and its freedom.

"The more touchstones one keeps safe,
the more handicaps one has."
Dr. Bak Nguyen

Simply put, all the precautions one will take to avoid trigging his or her touchstone is shaping his or her horizon, possibilities, and behaviors. And I told you that I do not believe that one should exorcist his or her touchstones. So are we stuck with them? All of them?

FEARS, **BELONGING**, and **FAILURES**, you will have to learn to live with those. Confidence, Love, Acceptance, and Speed will ease your way. What about the other touchstones?

DOUBT is the next in line. Doubting ourselves is a major source of stress and hormonal release. To doubt is not to be humble nor to be safe, but to re-question endlessly our choices and our actions.

Needless to say, the effect that has on your **ESTEEM**. Doubt will simply tank your confidence and break your horizon. Doubt has also the nasty habit of bringing the same problem again and again back on the table. We have all experienced how unpleasant doubt can be.

Well, can we get rid of doubt? Absolutely. Is it sane and safe to get rid of doubt? I'll let you to answer that one.

"Confidence is to make a call and be confortable to face its outcome. Arrogance is to think that there is no other way. "
Dr. Bak Nguyen

For those who think that being confident is to be arrogant, think again. In medicine, we all learned about the **educated guess**. We have a logic, a theory that we are looking to prove.

That being said, we are also keeping our eyes open to learn from the experience and to either verify our hypothesis or to replace it with a better one. The goal was not to be right but to get there gradually.

Using the same stratagem, why would one need to doubt? Make a call based on your preference, what you know at the moment, and be open to learn and to readjust on the way.

If you doubt the whole way through, you might mess up your own experiment and not gather the right data. This was an experiment, imagine something more serious...

> "Doubting will not help nor solve anything.
> Being flexible and aware will."
> Dr. Bak Nguyen

I told you that I am a sensitive soul born in an immigrant family looking to regain what they lost to the war. Well, I became a dentist for the love and pride of my parents. That being said, I still managed to find my passion in dental school, producing and directing an independent movie. By graduation, I had a shot to join Hollywood.

Well, don't ask me why, but I chickened out that one. Losing my brand new dental license was simply a price that I wasn't ready to pay. Then I came back to Montreal and open my own practice, with the hope to change the world…

We built a great and very futuristic clinic. I was physically present, every day, but my heart was burden with Hollywood regrets. After a year, I was facing bankruptcy. I was doubting myself.

Then, within months of running out of money, I signed a contract with myself, to become the best dentist I could be and not think of Hollywood for the next 10 years. Well, the rest is history.

Within months, I became a loved dentist. Today, people travel for hours to come in my dental chair. My company has become the hope of the renewal of dentistry. And no, I never went bankrupt.

What happened? How did I go from failure to success story? Well, by signing that contract with myself, I removed the doubts and regrets I have about my choices. That cleared the **SMOG** and I had the much needed clarity to embrace my patients.

You want more? Well, I got through these 10 years without looking back, wrap with success, love, and friendship, so much that I miss my exit date and 12 years had passed when I stopped and reopen my contract!

"Take doubt away and the odds of success
are now in your favor."
Dr. Bak Nguyen

I am not saying that everything went perfectly, but I was able to find a solution to each problem, and since that I am a dentist, my job is to fix people's problems, one at a time. With confidence, I change the world for the better, a smile at the time.

"Perfection is a lie."
Dr. Bak Nguyen

This is one of my favorite quotes. I am pretty sure that it came back at least 50 times within my 72 books. The next soft touchstone of stress is **PERFECTION**.

What is wrong with perfection? Well, it is because you are submitting your work to the opinion of all, with the liability that any criticism will have to be addressed. What do you think of the level of stress generated by such expectations?

I am a driver and an overachiever. I can tell you that perfection is a lie. Every time that something is perfect, it was made perfect in the narrative.

On the ground, people did the best with what was given and within the given time. Then, as History is written by the victors, others will be retelling a better tale of the events to perfection.

I do not believe in perfection. As an artist, as a businessman, as a philosopher, as a medical doctor, I never saw nor touched perfection. I often heard of it though. I believe in harmony.

This is how I struck down that touchstone from my board, looking for harmony instead of perfection. My works got propelled to the world stage with that philosophy, embracing harmony.

The big difference between harmony and perfection is that harmony is about melting with the surroundings and looking for synergy, while perfection was about being the best, being better than our surroundings.

Walk with me, which do you think makes a better leader, the perfect or the harmonious? And I am not a believer of compromise, I am a believer of logic and of results, but harmony made me an **Alpha**.

"The choice is very simple, are you looking
for pride or for peace?"
Dr. Bak Nguyen

And the best thing is that looking for harmony comes with very little stress. Again, I am not looking for compromise, but for harmony. I am looking to build bridges where it is possible. I am looking to connect and to empower. Every time I do so, my energy goes up and the fun is feeding my momentum.

On the contrary, looking for perfection, it is a matter of time before we *cannibalize* even those closest to us. We were looking to be THE ONE. Well, to me that is no fun at all and it is a lonely path. No thank you.

The third soft touchstone is **DENIAL**. This one is a little trickier. Denial is supposed to be a protective strategy to shield our soul from the hurt of the change or of a big loss. Should it fit in the hard touchstones? No, and here is why.

To be in denial, whatever the reason, is a choice that we make. We are postponing the storm of emotions for later. Well, guess what, the suppressed emotions locked away is steaming up and raising the pressure. The day it will blow, well, the emotions and the pain will be much worse than the initial shock.

Denial them their expression and they will grow until you will have no other choice than to live them completely and fully. Here, the life's examples are very personal, but I am sure that if you look in the mirror, you can find within your own examples, the confirmation of what I just shared with you. You won't have to look too far, just look for the first scar.

Denial is a choice. I respect your choice. Only you can choose but be advised that it will hurt either way. The longer the wait, the bigger the pain. Different, sure, but also bigger.

Having written many books on the **Quest of Identity**, I can assure you that whatever emotions and pain you deny, well, it will end up consuming most of your life force just to remain sealed. And the day it has consumed you entirely, well it will take control of what is left of your body and you will burst into flames, hurting those closest to you.

"I rather have the scar than to give it my life."
Dr. Bak Nguyen

In popular culture, we call those **DEMONS**. Demons are the emotions and pains one denies. Will you burst in flames? If you refuse the question, then those are the ones you will bear:

When will you burst in flames?
Who of those you loved will you hurt in the process?

It is never too late. For as long as you are still in control, that there is some life force left in you, you can release those demons and be finally free. Just make sure that you do so in a vast empty space, so no one will get hurt by the energy unleashed. That's the **vastness of the canvas**.

And the fourth soft touchstone? **Procrastination**.

Procrastination and denial are very similar. Procrastination is to be aware of the change, the emotions, and the consequences. You even have a reaction planned and you delay its execution.

Since the emotions are out already, well, you won't be nurturing a demon inside. The stress is a different one. Remember the **PSYCHOLOGICAL SMOG**? Well, you just add a new layer on top of what was laying there already.

To know that you have to do something and to keep it in your todo is a task in itself, one that also demands part of your life force and concentration. The worse part is that with the emotions long gone, you now have no motivation to act, just a task.

I told you that even what excites you today will eventually fade out and become a burden as you furnish your **PSYCHOLOGICAL SMOG**, well, I was referring to **PROCRASTINATION**.

"I am too lazy to have projects laying around in my mind."
Dr. Bak Nguyen

That's how I opened this journey with you. Well, that's my weapon and shield against procrastination: **LAZINESS**. People laugh when I introduce myself as a lazy person, they missed the point.

The words were more to my benefit, to remind me to stay ahead of stress and to escape the **SMOG**. That's my **LAZINESS**, that's also the source of my **MOMENTUM**.

A momentum coming for laziness. What a cool concept! But if I break it down to you, it makes much sense.

I see stress as a signal and a stimulus. Since I am a sensitive person, I know the power of my emotions and I also know that I do not control them. I can only choose to release them or to trap them away. Well, my emotions are part of myself, no way I am trapping myself. So I release them.

The change triggers a stimulus. I react by releasing my emotions. Now I have two problems to deal with: the change itself and my emotions.

Well, being a trained medical doctor showed me the way: to every problem, there is a remedy. I now have a reason to act (stimulus) and if I borrow the power of my emotions, I also have a free ride to start the journey. Free since I wasn't in control.

I know that the energy of my emotions will not last forever, so, very quickly, I do not sit on the free ride, but I run and build my speed from its shoulder to go even faster, running toward a solution. The feeling is a great one, an intoxicating one. That's how magic is created.

I grew addicted to that magic and air. I am so far ahead in such little time that all around me, it is vast and empty. It is calm, with no **SMOG**, no stress, no touchstone, just **serenity**.

That clarity is the ultimate of comforts. But soon enough, the **SMOG** will be catching up and I will have to repeat the process. Well, if you want the literal secret of my over achievements, here it is: I run on the shoulder of my emotions right when change was hot and triggering my touchstone. Doing so, I don't need to find motivation, since I use the stimulus. That's timing.

Then, I free the emotions that the stimulus is igniting and I surf the vibe to jump-start that journey. Again, that was the laziest way to face the situation.

Surfing, I built up my own speed to beat the fading of my emotions, creating my own air and speed: magic. That will take me way ahead into clarity.

And in **CLARITY**, well I easily found my answers looking at the horizon. Just like climaxing in sex, the sensation is extraordinary. From touching enlightenment to falling back into the arms of the **SMOG** catching up. I enjoy the rise and I enjoy the fall. And just like a teenager who just discovered the pleasure of his own body, well, I look forward to do it again and again.

What I can share with you is that the feeling never gets old and the sensation is always a great one. Try it once to understand, everyone has the right to happiness. Find your happiness discovering your worth, your heart, your mind, and your body.

And **PROCRASTINATION**? Climax once and you will see that there is simply no place for procrastination, so why delay the pleasure of a climax? It does simply not make sense.

This is why and how **DOUBT**, **DENIAL**, **PERFECTION**, and **PROCRASTINATION** are touchstones of stress, but not absolute touchstone. These you can get rid of without exorcism, without trauma. I call those the **MIRAGES**.

Choose what you see.

This is **TOUCHSTONE**, leveraging today's psychological smog.

STRESS is part of life, for better and for worse.
Better since it can be leveraged
Worse, if it is in control
Dr. BAK NGUYEN

CHAPTER 10

STRESSED LEARNING

by Dr. KEN SEROTA

Exposure to an acutely stressful event has numerous effects on learned behaviors and performance. It can impede learning to escape from an aversive stimulus, alter perseverative behavior, and thereby impede performance of a learning task.

What do such different responses to the same stressful events reveal about the true relationship between stress and learning, other than its apparent complexity?

First, it is unlikely that there are one or even two defining relationships between stress and learning. Second, they are not exclusively negative. Perhaps the capacity to respond in very different ways to stressful stimuli is the hallmark of a highly evolved and adaptive stress response. By appreciating, even capitalizing on its plasticity, it may be possible to more accurately describe relationships between stress and learning.

While learning during or immediately after the stress is often enhanced, stress disrupts memory retrieval and updating, and these effects are most pronounced for emotionally arousing material.

While stress around the time of learning is thought to enhance memory formation, thus leading to robust memories, stress markedly impairs memory retrieval, bearing, for instance, the risk of underachieving at exams.

From a scientific perspective of study, stress may hamper the updating of memories in the light of new information and induce a shift from a flexible, 'cognitive' form of learning towards rather rigid, 'habit'-like behavior.

The effects of stress on memory depend on the specific memory process investigated and the time between the stressful event and this memory process.

Emotionally arousing events are typically very well-remembered. Likewise, individuals who experienced extremely stressful (traumatic) events may suffer from very vivid memories of these events, suggesting that severe stress during or just before imprinting may boost memory formation.

The effects of stress on memory are, however, not limited to the formation of memories, but extend also to memory retrieval. Stress reduces the integration of new information into existing memories.

It affects not only how much is learned how memories are built. Stress cannot only affect how much information we learn and remember, but stress also flips the balance between the systems dominating learning and memory, which has considerable consequences for the nature and flexibility of memories and the goal-directedness of behavior.

To counteract the strong negative effects of stress on memory retrieval and updating stress reduction techniques or other coping strategies help to alleviate stress symptoms. Consider a patient being informed of the need for extensive treatment. The ecosystem at play in the dental office must be brought to the forefront. Stress arising from the treatment plan, the timeline, the cost can all be mitigated by referencing patient records, advisory considerations about situations, and conditions from the past.

Stress does not only induce a deficit in memory retrieval and memory updating, it also changes the way information is stored and retrieved by multiple memory systems.

The stress associated with case diagnosis and consultation may hinder the successful transfer of the information and reduce the patient's cognitive flexibility. However, the negative effects of stress on memory retrieval may be counteracted to some extent by thoroughly and repeatedly practicing useful routines which can be recalled rather automatically.

Oral hygiene instruction for children, a holistic health approach as part of the office culture, understanding the nature of postoperative pain, the awareness of immediate access in an emergency situation as a hallmark of a dental practice may be especially relevant in developing informed patients, compliant patients, and patient who shared their experiences as they are devoid of stress.

"We are under constant assault. We are adaptive,
we are resilient because of learned memory response."
Dr. Ken Serota

Being in the moment, centered, focused, grounded all contribute to remembering "things". The act of remembering minimizes stress, repeated tasks enhance memory capability. A life lived to the full is replete with memories. That should suffice as a need to accept stress, embrace it, and allow it to enable us to remember with joy.

This is **TOUCHSTONE**, leveraging today's psychological smog.

STRESS is part of life, for better and for worse.
Better since it can be leveraged
Worse, if it is in control
Dr. BAK NGUYEN

CHAPTER 11

LEVERAGE

by Dr. BAK NGUYEN

Now that we know that there are 7 touchstones of stress, 3 hard that we have to live with, and 4 mirages that our mindset can get rid of, what's next?

Well, the title of this book is **TOUCHSTONE, LEVERAGING TODAY'S PSYCHOLOGICAL SMOG**. The touchstones and the psychological smog, we covered. How about leveraging?

You heard right, how about leveraging? When I first met with Ken, he was astonished about my mindset and views, saying that I have a circular vision and as I zoom in, boom! To leverage is usually a word used in the financial world to express mechanisms to amplify one's outcome. It usually involves more risk as it promises a greater reward.

Leveraging also has a bad reputation. In the general crowd, it is often associated with **GREED**, **RISK**, and **GAMBLING**. The only point on which everyone agrees on is to leverage, one must be smart, or at least, smarter than the average.

I have no problem with leveraging. In fact, I am all about leveraging. I told you that I was a lazy guy looking for fun. Well, leveraging makes things much easier.

Am I smart enough to do so? Well, if I win, I have my answer. If I fail and survived the fall, I will have an edge and better inside of how it works and how to win next. If I do not survive, well, the story isn't mine to tell anymore.

About greed? Well, we are talking about ways to improve our lives and wellbeing, refusing to be victims to stress. How does greed apply to this situation? Greed is more.

We are looking for freedom and happiness, are we not, escaping from the grasp of stress? More freedom and more happiness, who will say no to that?

And what about the risk? It is sure that by leveraging, you will succeed? Unfortunately, no. But what is the alternative? To have 100% of the chance to remain victim to stress and to learn to survive it? Even at 1% chance of improvement, I will take the odds to improve my condition without blinking.

Rest assured, it is not as dramatic. The odds, if you are open to learn and to adapt are much more than 1%. The best thing is that the odds are always improving in your favor as you keep walking the journey. Ever heard the saying: "It does not get easier. You only get better"? This is what it is about, to leverage your conditions to improve on them. It all started with a choice, yours.

"Leverage your liabilities to move forward."
Dr. Bak Nguyen

This is one of my favorite quotes. I told you that I love fun, and fun I have as I grow, learn, and win, quickly. You came to know me as a **Momentum** or a Tornado, an overachiever saying that he is lazy and looking for fun. Well, let's break that down, shall we?

We now all know that speed will largely balance the effect of stress on a body, especially efficient to fight the stress of **FEAR**, **BELONGING**, and even of **ESTEEM**. Because I was lazy and looking for the easiest way out, I learned and mastered speed and momentum. Those are the leverages I took.

Then, as I gained in speed, I became a center of gravity, from the law of attraction. The more I achieve, the more changes happened around me. At first, the small wins caused much jealousy and bad mouths to vocal up.

My chance is that my speed was much greater and, as they finalized their first criticism, I was already way ahead, making their remarks obsolete. They hate me for that, but they quickly learn to hold their tongues to not look like fools.

Then, I kept pushing. Business, books, projects, and ideas. At first, my results were attracting people to me. Then, as my momentum kept growing, people were attracted by the promise of my potential and my next ideas. And I kept pushing, learning, growing, and adapting. Today, people are attracted to me simply for who I am.

Leveraging my speed, I got rid of the stress of perfection, of expectations, of belonging, of failure.

"Confidence is sexy."
Dr. Bak Nguyen

That keystone allowed me to break most of the barriers. And my confidence is sourcing from the love of my lover and best friend, Tranie Vo. Then, the birth of William doubled down on that love, and I rose higher and faster.

Look for **LOVE** and **CONFIDENCE**, those are the keystones that will be your leverage and the light you will need in any circumstances. Not everyone will have the chance to experience love right away.

That's ok. Be ready, prepare yourself, and work on your attraction. Who are you looking for? Well, you will have to attract that person of your dream, becoming better, wiser, gentler. That will build your confidence.

And as your confidence grow, now you are attractive, much more than you were. People can feel your presence. Don't be cocky, deep down, you are still the same person, only now, you are wearing the coat of confidence and its vibe. The trap of confidence is to lose control.

Confidence allows to keep doubts under control. Confidence will also grant you access to speed (no one insecure will ever embrace speed and leverage). Those are all **HOW**s. You still need to know the **WHAT** and the **WHY**. Those answers, you won't find in your head thinking. Those answers lay in your heart.

So the main difference between **CONFIDENCE** and **PRIDE** lays in the **HEART** and the other one lays in the **HEAD**. In simple words, keep your heart open and you will be confident and attractive. Live in your head and you will be the target of jealousy.

I told you that as I started, my small wins attracted more hate and jealousy. Well, it was because I was starting to rise and my peers were those within my initial condition. They hated me because from peers, I came to rise and they were not.

And the silly thing is that I had hard facts and results to prove my advancement. To prove... never fall for that trap, unless you are attracted to the **TOUCHSTONE OF BELONGING**.

This is not a golden rule, but one good enough to always keep close to your heart. Love, give, and do not look back. Ahead, that's you only chance to rise from the **SMOG**.

So I rose, leaving behind those talking and whispering. Then, I attracted mentors and people of experience looking into my ideas and my results. I have results, sure, but not the resources or knowledge to change the world, at least not yet. What the mentors loved was the potential. They joined my cause.

Now the big question was to know if I was ready to receive the help and the guidance. Trust me, if I was locked in my head, I would never keep the interest of my mentors, some created billions in value.

Humility and flexibility were the next keystones of my leveraging. Confidence was still the best of my asset, **PRIDELESS CONFIDENCE**.

"Funny thing, in the dictionary, the word PRIDELESS does not exist. If I just made up that word, it is my contribution of the day to make the world a better place."
Dr. Bak Nguyen

And then, I kept pushing with the support and guidance of my mentors. I became more, faster, and bolder. My world records writing books put the words on the table and my presence on the world map. Today, people are coming to me from all walks of life, looking for inspiration, for hope.

It is not about what I have, what I did, or what I am going to do anymore. It is about sharing a moment, a genuine moment. I finally manage to trick another major component of the **PSYCHOLOGICAL SMOG**, Time itself.

Maybe that's what Ken picked up on, saying that I was circular and not linear. With me, it is not about the past or the future, but about the present. My past opened the door to the connection. Whatever future we can build will depend on this present moment and its vibe. And that's how I invited Ken to change the world with me, from a dental chair.

The interviews are online, I invite you to look them up and to follow the process.

"When confidence and openness are, past, present, and future start to blend into one single vibe: possibility."
Dr. Bak Nguyen

If you were looking for a straight and single answer to the question of leveraging, mark down **PRIDELESS CONFIDENCE**. If you need more elaborations, it is about **CONFIDENCE, OPENNESS**, and **FLEXIBILITY**.

You won't have those looking in your head. You have to look for them in your heart.

"Confidence is sexy."
Dr. Bak Nguyen

As I attracted friends and mentors, you will be attracting them to. You attract what you are, alike and opposite. It is for you to learn to sort them out and to choose. Again, Confidence will be of much help here. So love to find love.

Is that all about leveraging? Or do you want some more? From **PRIDELESS CONFIDENCE**, you now have the means to overcome much of the **TOUCHSTONES OF STRESS**. How about more? About winning instead of avoiding?

We started this journey with the knowledge that stress is a stimulus that will cause a physiological hormonal reaction to allow us to either **FIGHT** or **FLEE**.

We covered the fleeing part, looking to avoid trigging the **TOUCHSTONES**. Fighting, I can tell you much about it, but I also told you that the better I became to struck down the walls, an even bigger one took immediately its place. So I am much too lazy to fight, and I tried that already. It is not working nor worth the effort.

So what is left if you do not want to either flee or flight something? Embrace it! As a dentist, I daily absorb the stress of my patients, that's how I became a loved doctor. How about doing the same for myself, for my own benefit?

I embrace each touchstone of stress as a stimulus opening the door to a journey. If I rush into that journey, I often control the terms of my engagement. Then, surfing on that advantage, I can gain more and more speed until I become the journey itself.

Speed is intoxicating and very charming. It will boost your confidence and your attractiveness, bringing more and more people to you. With that, fun and magic are lining up.

The alternative is to ignore that journey until we got forced into it. The price is still the same or even higher, but now the terms are now imposed. And must I tell you that the stress is much greater.

To have a good understanding of this phenomenon, the next time you are driving on the highway, look at your speed and tell me how do you feel. If you are driving at the average speed of the circulation, you do not feel anything, it is almost flawless, fluid.

Try to slow down and see how it feels. As you become the slowest driver on the highway, you will see the other cars passing you by, one after the next. Each passing by is adding up to your stress... try it and you will understand.

Now, try the other way around. As you were fluid with the circulation, speed up, drastically, and describe the feeling. It feels exhilarating until you pass by a police car...

Well, most of your journeys in life are pretty similar to that analogy. You can procrastinate and wait to be pushed in the lane to feel all the pressure of the ride on top of the pressure of being passed by and stressed out by the flow that you are obstructing.

Be with the flow and it feels like a normal ride. Speed up and surf on that flow and feel the magic. And you know what? In the journey of life, there are no such things as speed limits!

So if you ask me, I will embrace tension any day in remplacement to pressure.

"Tension and pressure are forces that you feel.
How do you experience it is about your speed
and position on the lane."
Dr. Bak Nguyen

This is why and how I embrace each stimulus coming my way. I sometimes even provoke them to see what will come out of it. This is what my mentors call being a driver and not just a doer. If you need a better description here it is, but be aware, this might upset some of you:

- **DRIVER**: ahead and speedy, master of leveraging
- **DOER**: going with the flow, balancing between stress and stimulus
- **THINKER**: procrastinating until pushed into the lane, victim of stress.

So which one are you? Nothing is set in stone, remember, you are the one choosing your fate and how you react to the stimuli of Life. And you can always change your mind later on. It is about action in the present and the future. The past, well, is passed.

"Prideless confidence and a taste for adventure, those are your best keystones to leverage yourself and to rise."
Dr. Bak Nguyen

It all boils down to how you choose to see Life. It is an **OPPORTUNITY**? You are feeling tension and the excitement of discovering a new journey.

Is it **CHANGE**? You are feeling the obligation to react. Will it be fun or a responsibility, it will be up to how you make up your mind. Know that the outcome will often be related to how you decided to see the change, to begin with. Pressure versus Tension.

Is it **FORCED**? Well, in this case, you will feel the full weight of the burden, often with much handicaps since you have postponed the unavoidable until you have no other choice.

If you were in denial, well you never prepared for what's ahead. If you were preparing for a long time, well, let's hope that what you prepared for is what you will experience on the way. If not, can you unlearn to relearn quickly? It's all about how you see Life.

"Embrace Life and see it as an opportunity.
That's your leverage."
Dr. Bak Nguyen

This is **TOUCHSTONE**, leveraging today's psychological smog.

STRESS is part of life, for better and for worse.
Better since it can be leveraged
Worse, if it is in control
Dr. BAK NGUYEN

CHAPTER 12

COVID FATIGUE

by Dr. BAK NGUYEN

I could not end this journey without addressing that issue, one that my co-author Dr. Serota holds pretty close to his heart. What about the COVID-fatigue and its effects on stress?

I am not sure that I am the right person to answer the question, but here is my take. During COVID time, I was under more stress than I never experienced in my life. I am saying that because COVID put me in the seat of a **victim reacting**. I remained so for the first 2 weeks, waiting and reacting.

Then, I learned that the confinement will be for another month or more. That should have put me out of my misery with a heart attack as the CEO of an expanding company and millions of dollar on the line. At the edge and very depressed, I realized that I was simply not myself, waiting, and reacting. I am more a provoking kind of guy.

As I decided that everything not in my control is simply none of my business to care, I even stopped following the daily lives about the update on the COVID crisis. I went the other way and looked for influence.

As soon as I found some relevancy and influence (purpose), I felt different. I was back at my usual self, leveraging tension instead of falling victim to pressure. That was a major shift within COVID.

From looking for ways to save the economy and local commerces, to fighting an amateur mayor using the metropolis as an eco-friendly experiment to ease the tension of Black Lives Matters to hosting the **INTERNATIONAL ALPHAS DENTAL SUMMITS**, I was there at every turn.

Well, we had our victories and our defeats, but never the burden of stress was an issue. Then, I got the green light to resume clinical duty and to conformed to the new improvised norms of safety. With the assistance of my COO, Tranie Vo, and of my whole team, we led the coming back.

Within the days prior to reopening, we were out on the field looking to gap the shortage of PPE (Personal Protective Equipment). On that matter, we helped local clinics to reopen in time. We covered those on-air, within the **ALPHASHOW**.

Then, it was about reassuring the team and to coordinate the coming back. My team of human resources took care of that part. My role as the leader and figurehead of the company was to reassure the patients, which I did.

The whole summer, I was front and center to greet them and to take care of them while mentoring my protege dentists throughout the chaos.

We did what was possible, but I can assure you that all of the patients were happy to be received and left with a smile. Was it mission accomplished?

Well, I told you that I was in the middle of an expansion, so we have to work with the banks to restructure that deal and the delay of construction so it reflects the new reality, the ever changing new reality. Millions were at stake.

And in the midst of all of that, people started to cave to stress, falling victims to stress and depression. We lost a few of our team members in that sense. We dealt with each situation swiftly to accommodate and to limit the collateral damages.

All of this while swimming through the financials of the government's requirement for grant and loans, and doing my best to keep my relevancy on my board of directors, for the next phase of **Mdex & Co**'s expansion. At stake were hundreds of millions in investment.

Is that enough as stress? To avoid litigation, I also had to pay in full 3 months of rent during lockdown with no revenue in. All of this while writing more books and setting more world records, faster than ever. Does that make any sense?

Well, it does. Every time I faced a wall, I needed the energy to climb above that wall, to dig under, or to strike it down. That takes energy and motivation. Especially when you know that the next wall, higher and ticker, is right around the corner. **MORALE** is the only keystone that will give you a fighting chance.

So I protected and feed my **MORALE** looking daily for the next win, as small as it could be. Each victory boosts my confidence and esteem and from that esteem, I renewed my hope to keep pushing for the next win.

Soon enough, I gained in speed and led the way. One victory after the next. That's why and how I scored writing a book every 8 days for 8 weeks straight to reach the world record of writing **72 books over 36 months**, publishing 6 books within a month, and getting drafted by **Barnes and Noble**. My tornado was now a force to be wrecking with.

And at home? Well, the other danger of confinement was to run out of air and to burst our stress and frustration with those we love the most. I was very aware of the danger. During the first 2 weeks of confinement, Tranie just got out of surgery, so I was the attending nurse, home, taking care of her and of William.

I learned to cook and to nurture while waiting for life to resume. As stress and frustration were building up, I went out walking, even on cold rainy days. I doubled down on kindness, patience, and generosity with those I loved, even if I felt different inside.

Playing music became a stress reliever, one I held on to as a lifesaver. For the 2 months in confinement, I even shared, once a week, some of these moments with my audience on social media, having them listen to a private concert from my living room.

I can tell you that 8 months after the facts, I am closer than ever with my family, Tranie, William, and my parents as we came to appreciate each moment we have.

> *"Kindness, patience and generosity."*
> Dr. Bak Nguyen

And fatigue? Well, I must tell you that by October, after 7 months running without rest, I felt the exhaustion. I took 12 days off to readjust. Surprise, I may not had a schedule during those 12 days home, but I kept producing interviews, **ALPHASCLASS**.

This is when I launched a new series, **THE INNOVATORS**, and interviewed RON KLEIN, the inventor of the magnetic stripe of the credit card, **MLS**, and the person who digitalized **WALL STREET's BOND MARKET**.

Well, it wasn't working since it wasn't scheduled. I simply had fun enjoying myself and connecting with people. And you know what? I felt so good to not have a schedule and be a slave reacting. That took much of the remaining stress away.

So what I learned, is that it is good to plan ahead, but be aware of its negative effects. Now, I try to keep the planning to the minimum, knowing that it will come back soon enough. To do so, I must be aware, flexible, and very creative. That I am, so why deprive myself of the fun of the moment?

And fatigue? Well, the fun of scoring each victory kept me going. The relief of stress from throwing away the schedule and the organizer took care of the rest.

TODAY, I found my footing with my new reality, one that required of me, not twice but 10 times what I was doing before. I am fine with that. I am ready.

Just to prove to you the adaptation it required. Prior to **COVID**, I was a CEO, and full-time dentist, and a world record writer. While in confinement, I became a nurse, a full-time father, an handicapped CEO, a host, and an anchor. While I kept writing books, some were international collaborations with experts form all around the world.

My most collaborative book has 14 doctors joining in, from several countries. That was a lot of communication, back and forth. Believe it or not, it was part of my 6 publishing books to Amazon, from the end of July to the end of August. Where there is a will, there is a way.

Was that stressful? Well, they were great stimuli, and you all know what I do with stimuli. I use them to propel myself.

Eat well, sleep well. Be kind, be open, be aware. Then, swallow your pride and be flexible to adapt, every day. What was good yesterday may become your burden today. Look for your next victory as fast as possible and readjust from there.

No doubt, do your best with what is given and move on. You failed? Acknowledge the failure, learn, and move on. Live is happening ahead, if there is one absolute truth, well this is one. Move on and look ahead.

And finally fatigue? Well, the fun on the way will counterbalance your fatigue, if you listen to your body and physiological needs, food, sleep, sex, hormones, and security.

This is the closest I can come up with as a recipe and a testimonial all in one. May you find your fun ahead, discovering what you are made of and embracing your inner powers. With words like those, no stress will ever strike you down.

This is **TOUCHSTONE**, leveraging today's psychological smog.

CHAPTER 13

SUBJECTIVE OVERLOAD

by Dr. KEN SEROTA

It is endlessly more exciting to have bountiful options to choose from, the quintessential candy store mentality. However, a cornucopia of choice affecting the decision-makers' motivations, desires, and impulsiveness can result in a skewed perception leading to consequences. We make choices based on subjective knowledge.

By way of example, people who feel unknowledgeable are invariably prone to **purchase** when more choice options are available, which is consistent with the notion of **more is better**. This pattern is reversed for people who feel knowledgeable.

They are influenced by due diligence of the features of the available choices, thus their subjective knowledge mitigates the desire to **go whole hog**.

COVID-19 has created a negativistic period wherein the mental health of dentists has been impacted upon with profound implications. Elevated levels of subjective overload and psychological distress among dentists can differ for social, financial, cultural, and environmental reasons.

We all have choices in the manner by which we respond to stressors taking these variables into account. Information on the contagion comes from multiple avenues and we must process them all independently in order to arrive at a consensus.

Factor in the needs of our families and our team members, it becomes a daunting challenge fraught with crevices and chasms.

In order to minimize the long-term effects of psychological distress, due to subjective overload, our profession may require **mental health workshops for dentists** in order to reduce personal and professional fears associated with the health risks of the pandemic.

As well, the ramifications of lockdown, financial reversals, and the recognition that what we knew is no longer, raise the level of primal fear, the fear of the unknown.

The same holds true for our team members as they must contend with the deluge of information pertaining to innovative infection-control methods which might provide a sense of safety, and in turn, might reduce psychological distress and subjective overload. Their job descriptions and positions have been recalibrated with the attendant unease of uncertainty about their future.

And yet, if the challenges we face don't scare us, then they are probably not important. COVID should cause us fear. It is a demon that wears many disguises. We are frightened for ourselves, for our family.

Unseen, it is an implacable foe and in far too many cases an invincible enemy. We are cognitively deluged from every corner. Our goal is not to find the perfect solution to control it or to save ourselves from its ravaging onslaught, but rather **to better our approach** from day to day and avoid a cataclysmic overload.

In order to address subjective overload, it is essential to find clarity, meaning, and fulfillment. We can't allow the noise to force us to give up. We need to build the world we can see for itself, not encased in sound and artifice, even if others can't see it.

"Listen to your own drum and your drum only.
It's the one that makes the sweetest sound."
Dr. Ken Serota

We have to unite as one in our personal and professional lives. We must learn to understand one another and if there's any hope of us understanding each other, we have to learn to listen. To create a space in which the other person feels heard. The subjective overload is mitigated.

Accept the difficulty in identifying, understanding or empathizing with those who have embraced the noise. Their opinions invariably differ from ours and in and of itself that is okay, we are all entitled to our own unique belief system.

Our cultures have created a fork in the road of our minds. Our ability to listen has been subjugated by the cacophony of sounds and sight designed to vaccinate us from reason and logic.

"Independence of mind and thought is difficult
to control in whatever context."
Dr. Ken Serota

Thus we must begin to truly listen, actively listen. Recognize our reactions, how our response manifests, and from where. We all have a story that we embrace, regardless of perceptions at the time. Subjective overload colors everything we do and any state of time.

Acceptance of our emotional responses is the most important thing. Self-care and compassion are essential in a world where sensory and cognitive assault serves the ends of others.

If we choose to come together then we can create a bulwark of humanity wherein we can bridge our differences and listen independent of the noise and understand in spite of the message delivered by others.

"Trust is not born out of what we do well,
rather it is born out of what we believe."
Dr. Ken Serota

This is our strength as it pertains to cognitive distortion and subjective overload. If we inspire others with our thoughts, then our heart wins and defeats the stressor and its impact on our spiritual and corporeal selves. We must assume personal leadership.

Leadership is not a journey to rise in the ranks of self, rather leadership is a journey to help those around us rise in deference to the noise from a world outside of our control. If we talk ownership of our independent thoughts, then we can share them with ours looking for help.

"The value of our lives is not determined by what we do for ourselves, it is determined by what we do for others."
Dr. Ken Serota

It is a naturally occurring pattern, grounded in the biology of human decision making, which explains why we are inspired by some people, leaders, messages, and organizations over others. If we determine to whom we should listen, then subjective overload is manageable.

Considering all the factors that could influence our responsiveness, the key factor as referenced, is trust. In the midst of the cannonade, we need to see the bigger picture, drown out the noise, hear our own song, and and sing it with gusto and relish.

Our inability to analyze the meaning of the noise leads to frustration or guilt. You lose the ability to respond with healthy accountability in the midst of the overload. It is hard to separate our emotions from what is factually true or untrue when the sound and fury is overwhelming.

Have we set clear expectations of what we want or need? Do we have the support or resources to enable us to respond or perform?

We need to become our own guide, rather than be guided, use our imagination and creativity rather than accept anyone else's direction.

"One of the things an infinite mindset provides is a calm confidence."
Dr. Ken Serota

Those of us who embrace an infinite mindset can actually come out of hard times better off than when we entered. It is not the strong that survive, it's the adaptable.

The subjective overload omnipresent in our lives is controllable. When we are accepting, radically or otherwise, the noise will lessen, the melody will become less discordant and invariably, it will fade into the distance.

This is **TOUCHSTONE**, leveraging today's psychological smog.

STRESS is part of life, for better and for worse.
Better since it can be leveraged
Worse, if it is in control
Dr. BAK NGUYEN

CHAPTER 14

TODAY

by Dr. BAK NGUYEN

TODAY, that's the last word of the title that we haven't addressed yet. Since this is not an article, writing about today has the liability that it will expire pretty soon. We won't want that since the content of this book is timeless.

That being said, **TODAY** is **COVID** time. Post-TODAY, life will be drastically different. And the stress? Stress will only be amplified by an X factor, in the midst of the COVID war and post-COVID.

You do not agree? What do you think will happen after COVID, are we having more human contacts or less physical contacts? Already our society was suffering from a lack of human physical touch, the rise of the massage industry will confirm my affirmation, and massage is not sex, it is about nurturing and feeling of being at the center of the attention for a moment.

So now that half or more of our lives will be virtual, that even sex might move digitally, how we will purge our hormones sitting on the same chair, looking at the same screen for school, work, entertainment, friendship, and even sex?

This is no secret, some of the most visited sites on the web are porn sites. Now that bars and clubs are closing, the meeting and hookup websites are spiking. That's the initial fun, but then what? Looking at profiles and pictures to choose our next one night or our next mate?

This might seem efficient and easy, but the reset and next buttons are also complicating the situation since there is no real engagement. Our body will either be craving the hormones we usually produced in social interactions, while stress and drama won't go away... and we will end up stocking even more stress hormones with nowhere to flee or to purge.

Unless the cure for COVID is to run a mile every day, our problems at the beginning of this journey are just getting worse.

Meeting with our teachers, friends, boss, and colleagues will also happen more and more from the same window we are now allowed to use. The deluxe size is a 16-17 inched display, unless you have hooked it up to a giant display, that's the normal wisdom size to the new world.

The on-the-go size is closer to 5-6 inches, in the palm of our hand. The same window, but much smaller. If we know that the window is narrowing down, do you think that more or less information will be transferred through that opening? Logic will tell you lesser and lesser. The information will sort out itself as some will be more predominant than others. And who will be doing the sorting?

Before I answer that question, what happened in the last decade as smartphones connected everyone? Social media surged. And what is dominant on social media? Drama, jealousy and fake news.

Within the second half of the last decade, some have even tailored their lives on the pictures they could see and post on social media. Some extremists even paid the ultimate price for a great picture!

I am not making that up, just search the news and the archives and you will find those articles and sad events. So if before we were living in a magazine and a customer catalog, **TODAY**, we are living on our own catalog of a 6 inches screen scrolling for 3 seconds or less. And we are defining ourselves from that size.

Needless to say that the speed is only going up and that comparison will be stacking on in volume. Until now, I told you that the remedy to some stress touchstones was speed. That is only true when you are running faster than the average living around you.

Now with the advent of 5G, with 1 minute video, 280 characters, an update from the previous limit of 140 characters to express ourselves, the steam is rising in a smaller and smaller content, that 6-inch window.

How fast can our body evolve to catch up with that shift in living? This is the **anthropologic EL NINO** of our generation. Who will survive and who will go extinct? It is not just life that is changing, but the conditions in which we are living at the biochemical level, our hormones to start with.

And what is happening while the major shift is operating, pushed by **FEAR** and **COVID**? We are drowning in our **PSYCHOLOGICAL SMOG**, chasing our tail.

"Rise up to clarity and you will all see what is coming next."
Dr. Bak Nguyen

What a poor job I am doing helping you to reduce your stress level. But the theme of this chapter was **TODAY**... Well, there are fights that we cannot win, in those cases, follow the flow and surf the change.

They are other fights that we can and must win to keep our sanity and relevancy. I am talking about our **happiness** and **freedom**.

I told you that **COVID** propelled my work and reputation on the world stage as I became a world anchor in my field. Even if I was present on social media before **COVID**, by the confinement, that was the only place I could go, safely.

But then, I remembered a golden rule of psychology: every time you connect, the energy is going up. Otherwise, you compare and the energy is spiralling down. That's how I embraced social media in **COVID** times, looking for connections.

Within a few hours, THE ALPHAS were born. The name came much later, but the genuine connections and friendships that found the ALPHAS started right away within the first connections, Dr. PAUL OUELLETTE, Dr. ERIC LACOSTE, Dr. PAUL DOMINIQUE and Dr. JULIO REYNAFARJE.

Each of these interviews were recorded and available on my website and the major social outlets. If you want to know how you can use that 6 or 15 inches window to create connections, I invite you to have a look at those interviews. They are unscripted, uncut and you can see how strangers came to leverage social media to create lasting bonds and friendships.

From there, I leveraged social media as a streaming platform to communicate our views and visions and to recruit more like-minded leaders.

Today, **THE ALPHAS** have members all around the world. Those members are shakers and difference makers. Our summits and discussions have the impact to ease the transition ahead in economy and health.

Were there drama and jealousy? Of course, it won't be a human story without those, but **SPEED** and **ACHIEVEMENTS** kept me ahead. The bumps on the road remain as such, bumps on the road long passed behind me. Now, they became anecdotes and footnotes.

How many of you can tell me a similar story, one of how you made new friends and brought the hope to change the world from social media? It was possible because I use social media as a 2 ways communication streak.

I will be lying if I told you that I have no stress from social media. My stress is primarily related to the stability and the speed of my internet connexion. Every time I am going live, that is a toll on my spirit.

"I remain very hopeful since amongst all the stress possible, my internet connexion was my main concern."
Dr. Bak Nguyen

So that's how I leveraged today **PSYCHOLOGICAL SMOG** to my advantage, to flee from the reality of confinement, only to find a better way to, not fight it, but to surf it.

I told you that I am preparing round 2 of my media presence. That round is called **THE ALPHACLASS**, my version of the masterclass. Well, until lately, to present a seminar, we needed to be physically present. Well, the reality of **COVID** removed those barriers.

TODAY, I can have experts from anywhere in the world to be part of my summits and **ALPHACLASS**. My audience too, has now grown international.

To the saying that none is a prophet in his own village, we found a way to beat that one, since the village has expanded to the four corners of the globe, diluting much the naysayers and the jealousy.

And our **SUMMITS** and **ALPHACLASSES** are of international caliber.

"Leverage your liability to move forward."
Dr. Bak Nguyen

That's how I leveraged my confinement, the lockdown, and social media. I traded in most of the touchstones of stress for genuine connections and hope. The only stress-related is now the speed of my internet connexion.

Use the internet as a means to connect and to boost productivity, not to consume more while not being sure of the source and quality of what you are consuming.

The world may have changed, but we haven't, at least not yet. So online, what is foreseeable is our behaviors and habits, forging the fabric of neuronal connections... of social behavior.

Just be aware that online, most people did not transpose their normal social behaviors and boundaries, saying what they want with not much filters nor reflections... action - reaction will establish a new alternate reality.

Compare, and you are looking down. And where ever you are looking, is also where you are heading. Connect and look up, and you might have a chance to rise.

Social media gave us a new way to connect and communicate. How we choose to use it is up to us. Just be aware of our actions and be prepared for the reactions to our actions. Then, we will be reacting to the reaction, establishing consequences.

Both parties now will have to deal with the consequences of our actions and reactions. That will establish a trend. If that trend is left untouched for long enough, it will become a new norm, a new reality.

By itself, there is no stress element to this, but how we are receiving the data and information that we are generating ourselves.

"For as long as you are reacting, you a late in the chain."
Dr. Bak Nguyen

This is what I meant by saying that there are price and terms to every deal. Reacting, we are victims and are assuming the pressure. Pro-acting, even provoking, we are pushing the change with our terms, trading pressure for tension instead.

So what is stress? A stimulus. How and where are we positioning ourselves toward the stimulus will define our experience as either positive or negative. React and you are a victim, that can't be positive.

What social media and COVID brought to the table is the acceleration of the trends, the underlined habits, and the acceleration of the consequences. If you are ahead, social media and COVID will propel you.

If you have your head underwater waiting and reacting, well, social media and COVID are the perfect storm to your worse nightmare.

This is **TOUCHSTONE**, leveraging today's psychological smog.

STRESS is part of life, for better and for worse.
Better since it can be leveraged
Worse, if it is in control
Dr. BAK NGUYEN

CONCLUSION

by Dr BAK NGUYEN

This is the end. Hold your breath and count to ten... Really?! Seriously, I have a hard time believing that this is already the end of our journey together, is stress ever ending?

And to that question, you have your answer: it depends on how you are seeing stress and how to decide to react to it. What amazed me is that what seems to be true and unmovable today, eventually will be something that will fade away so much that we might have a hard time remembering it. What does that tell you?

That everything will pass, so this one will too. Until the next one arrives. I told you before, this is how Life works, changing, and morphing. If your interpretation of Life is change and that you are afraid of that same change, well, you are in for a long ride...

If you are seeing change as an opportunity, a window to escape your reality, to surf your vision, or to simply have fun, well, the changes were not stressful at all, the changes were stimuli inviting you to be part of something great, something exciting!

"Your perspective of Life will define the degree of stress you are experimenting with."
Dr. Bak Nguyen

And the first thing to understand is that **guilt** and **shame** won't help you here. Neither are **doubts** and the **pressure** of pleasing to belong. We are what we are. We can grow it, we can ignore it, we can cultivate it or we can amputate it, it is part still you.

My place here is not to judge, but to share with you my perspective. I am not a believer of amputations, plain and simple. So, to exorcist your fears and demons won't be my approach of predilection.

Instead, I will invite you to embrace who you are, the good and the lesser, and to come to terms with yourself. You alone can do that, you alone, and do it alone since the presence of anybody else will contaminate the purpose of the exercise and set you back.

Whatever you like, use it, enjoy it. What you do not like, let it lay around as a decor in the corner. You will eventually completely forget about it or leverage on it somehow to further yourself.

If you still need convincing, what will you feed to the fire in the chiminea first? The furniture you like or the extras laying around? There is always a use to everything. How do you think that I find my inspiration writing books? Well, those liabilities laying around were sometimes great stories to share.

I do not talk about my fears. I told you that and will advise you to think twice before you do. I kept leveraging on them. Today, my worst fear is to show up in front of God unworthy of the gifts and talents I received.

Well, that does not mean that I am spending my life in fear. Actually, on the contrary, I have found a way to postpone most of my fears into the next Life, living this one almost unfearful. If you want the whole story, I will refer you to my first book, **SYMPHONY OF SKILLS**, in which I dedicated a whole chapter on the matter.

But this is fear, not stress! Well, take away fear and most of the stress has been rendered inactive. Now, it is easier to see stress for what it really is, a stimulus. If there is one thing to take from this book, this is it:

"Stay away from fear and stress is almost gone!"
Dr. Bak Nguyen

Easier said than done. But going through the breaking down of the **TOUCHSTONES OF STRESS**, we now know that they are hard ones (which you might have to deal with) and soft ones, the mirages (which you can get rid of with the right mindset).

As I was addressing stress in a large sense and leveraging my own experience to show you how I leveraged myself from those stimuli, Ken approached this stress as a surgeon, zooming on the problem.

Ken addressed the **TOUCHSTONES OF STRESS** from the specific perspective of the dental professional. From the next tools to the next work environment, how can stress be relieved from our daily or be fuelled if we do not understand the tools we have in hand.

Even if Dr. Serota was talking from the dental chair, his approach to stress can easily be extended for general purposes. If teledentistry is about dentistry, the adaptation to the new technology and to leverage our success, or to be intimidated are common themes.

I really hope that you found inspiration and some answer to your remedy to stress, especially, in modern times.

I would like to thank Dr. Serota to have inspired the subject of stress for this journey, my 73rd book. Writing with Ken was a wonderful surprise as we both started from different points of view and style, but joining forces and progressing, our words and chapters were finishing the other's sentence.

This proves one point: that stress is universal and so are its remedy. It might not be a one-size-fits-all, but the core is pretty much the same no matter your culture, your beliefs, your ages, and your backgrounds. **Touchstones** and **keystones**.

Stress is something that is deeply rooted in our DNA. But stress can also be an expired label from another age… now you have the keys to your own liberation, if you choose so.

Oh, and one last thing:

"If you want a sure keystone to defeat stress, look for fun. "
Dr. Bak Nguyen

This is **TOUCHSTONE,** leveraging today's psychological smog.

STRESS is part of life, for better and for worse.
Better since it can be leveraged
Worse, if it is in control
Dr. BAK NGUYEN

ABOUT THE AUTHOR

From Canada, **Dr BAK NGUYEN**, Nominee Ernst and Young Entrepreneur of the year, Grand Homage Lys DIVERSITY, and LinkedIn & TownHall Achiever of the year. Dr Bak is a cosmetic dentist, CEO and founder of Mdex & Co. His company is revolutionizing the dental field. Speaker and motivator, he wrote 72 books over 36 months accumulating many world records (to be officialized).

- **ENTREPRENEURSHIP**
- **LEADERSHIP**
- **QUEST OF IDENTITY**
- **DENTISTRY AND MEDICINE**
- **PARENTING**
- **CHILDREN BOOKS**
- **PHILOSOPHY**

In 2003, he founded Mdex, a dental company upon which in 2018, he launched the most ambitious private endeavour to reform the dental industry, Canada wide. Philosopher, he has close to his heart the quest of happiness of the people surrounding him, patients and colleagues alike. In 2020, he launched an International collaborative initiative named THE ALPHAS to share knowledge and to Entrepreneurs and Doctors to thrive through the Greatest Pandemic and Economic depression of our time.

In 2016, he co-found with Tranie Vo, Emotive World Incorporated, a tech research company to use technology to empower happiness and sharing. U.A.X. the ultimate audio experience is the landmark project on which the team is advancing, utilizing the technics of the movie industry and the advancement in ARTIFICIAL INTELLIGENCE to save the book industry and to upgrade the continuing education space.

These projects have allowed Dr Nguyen to attract interests from the international and diplomatic community and he is now the center of a global discussion in the wellbeing and the future of the health profession. It is in that matter that he shares his thoughts and encourages the health community to share their own stories.

"It's not worth it go through it alone! Together, we stand, alone, we fall."

Motivational speaker and serial entrepreneur, philosopher and author, from his own words, Dr Nguyen describes himself as a dentist by circumstances, an entrepreneur by nature and a communicator by passion. He also holds recognitions from the Canadian Parliament and the Canadian Senate.

www.DrBakNguyen.com

From Canada, **Dr KEN SEROTA**, DDS, MMSc, graduated from the University of Toronto Faculty of Dentistry in 1973 and received his Certificate in Endodontics and Master of Medical Sciences degree from the Harvard-Forsyth Dental Center in Boston, Massachusetts. He was awarded the George W. Switzer Memorial Award for excellence in prosthodontics in 1973. In 1981, he was awarded the American Association of Memorial Award in Research. In 1987 he was awarded the Ontario Dental Association for contribution to continuing education.

In 2000, he founded ROOTS, the first online Endodontic forum and coordinated the first ROOTS Summit. In 2004, in concert with Oemus Media, he founded the Roots Journal. In 2015 he founded NEXUS, in order to integrate all dental disciplines. Contributing editor to Endodontic Practice, he has published over 70 articles and has lectured internationally on endodontics and implants. He is the Global Director of Social Media and Marketing for Navident and is a clinical instructor in the University of Toronto postdoctoral endodontics department.

Dr. Serota is a member of : Ontario Dental Association, Halton Peel Dental Association, Canadian Dental Association, Ontario Society of Endodontists, American Association of Endodontists, Alpha Omega Fraternity, Digital Dental Society.

He coordinates the annual Run for the Cure event, to bring an end to cancer.

UAX

ULTIMATE AUDIO EXPERIENCE

A new way to learn and enjoy Audiobooks. Made to be entertaining while keeping the self-educational value of a book, UAX will appeal to both auditive and visual people. UAX is the blockbuster of the Audiobooks.

UAX will cover most of Dr Bak's books, and is now negotiating to bring more authors and more titles to the UAX concept. Now streaming on Spotify, Apple Music and available for download on all major music platforms. Give it a try today!

www.DrBakNguyen.com

FROM THE SAME AUTHOR
Dr Bak Nguyen

www.DrBakNguyen.com

MAJOR LEAGUES' ACCESS

BUSINESS

CHILDREN'S BOOK
with William Bak

The Trilogy of Legends

DENTISTRY

LIFESTYLE

QUEST OF IDENTITY

MILLION DOLLAR MINDSET

THE POWER OF YES 2 -036
VOLUME TWO: SHAPELESS
BY Dr BAK NGUYEN

THE POWER OF YES 3 -039
VOLUME THREE: LIMITLESS
BY Dr BAK NGUYEN

075 - **THE POWER OF YES 4**
VOLUME FOUR: PURPOSE
BY Dr BAK NGUYEN

076 - **THE POWER OF YES 5**
VOLUME FIVE: ALPHA
BY Dr BAK NGUYEN

077 - **THE POWER OF YES 6**
VOLUME SIX: PERSPECTIVE
BY Dr BAK NGUYEN

TITLES AVAILABLE AT

www.DrBakNguyen.com

AMAZON - BARNES & NOBLE - APPLE BOOKS - KINDLE
SPOTIFY - APPLE MUSIC

DR.

Bak Nguyen